The Smart Guide to

Word

2000

Further Skills

Also available from Continuum:

Morris: *The Smart Guide to Word 2000 Basic Skills*
Muir: *The Smart Guide To Windows 2000 Professional*
McBride and McBride: *The Smart Guide to Access 2000 Basic Skills*
McBride: *The Smart Guide to Access 2000 Further Skills*
Weale: *The Smart Guide to Excel 2000 Basic Skills*
Weale: *The Smart Guide to Excel 2000 Further Skills*

Coles and Rowley: *Word 97 Basic Skills*
Coles and Rowley: *Word 97 Further Skills*

The Smart Guide to

Word 2000

Further Skills

**A Progressive Course
for New Users**

Stephen Morris

CONTINUUM

London · New York

Continuum

The Tower Building, 11 York Road, London SE1 7NX

370 Lexington Avenue, New York, NY 10017-6550

First Published 2001

British Library Cataloguing-in-Publication Data
A CIP record for this book is available from the British Library.

ISBN 0-8264-5698-7

Typeset by Butford Technical Publishing, Birlingham, Worcs.
Printed and bound in Great Britain by Creative Print and Design, Wales

Contents

Acknowledgments

Windows and Word 2000 © Microsoft Corporation, all rights reserved. Screen displays from Word 2000 reprinted with permission from Microsoft Corporation.

This book is based on *Word 97 Further Skills* by Sue Coles and Jenny Rowley.

About this book

Aims

This book is intended for users of Word 2000 who already have a working knowledge of the package and wish to progress further to improve both their productivity in document production and the quality of documents produced.

You can use it:

❑ As part of a college course

❑ For independent study

❑ For reference

Although this book uses a business-oriented approach for the practical activities, this approach will be easily adaptable to other situations where documents for other purposes, such as assignments or projects, are being produced.

It is assumed that you are familiar with the following activities in Word 2000:

❑ Text formatting: fonts, margins, alignment, basic bullets and numbering

❑ Navigating around a document; working with more than one document

❑ Moving, copying, deleting, and finding and replacing text

❑ Tabs and tables

❑ Borders and shading

If you need to brush up on these skills, you may find it useful to refer to *Word 2000 Basic Skills*, which provides an introduction to Word 2000 and assumes no prior knowledge of word processing.

A note to lecturers and students

This book explores advanced word processing techniques through a series of applications-orientated exercises. The approach is structured to focus on the end product, whether that product be a report, Web page, manuscript or other document. A series of self-contained sessions takes students through the production of various document types and introduces them to the more advanced features and functions of the word processing package. Each session comprises a series of exercises. As each new function is introduced, the book explains both why the function is useful and how to use it.

The approach is designed not only to extend students knowledge of Word but also to offer them a conceptual framework for word processing that will facilitate the development of transferable skills.

The learning material requires little, if any, input by lecturers, and can therefore be used in programmes based on independent learning. Students learn by practising the commands and techniques to produce specific types of documents.

Word 2000 is a sophisticated package including many desktop publishing type features, a graphics package and a draw package. The text is selective and does not deal with all these in detail, but does take students step-by-step to an advanced level at which they can explore other features when they are needed.

The exercises follow a theme. The majority of documents relate to an estate agency and a wide variety of documents are developed. Early exercises create documents that are reused later in the book.

In Word there are often many ways of achieving the same operation. This book offers the quickest and most user friendly means of achieving set objectives. Although at times other methods may also be indicated, preference is given to operations based on the use of the mouse and menu options. This approach makes maximum use of the self-explanatory nature of the menu options and dialog boxes, and does not ask the user to remember key combinations. Key combinations are indicated against menu options in the system, and users may familiarise themselves with these as their experience in using the software develops.

The appendix, *Customising Word*, is intended for:

❏ Those whose Word system has been customised so that it does not use the default settings assumed in this book. (Students should ask lecturers to perform the necessary commands to return their system to its default setting.)

❏ Those students who, having worked through all the units in the book, feel confident enough to create their own settings for Word.

Conventions

The following conventions have been adopted to distinguish between the various objects on the screen:

❏ On-screen buttons and icon names are shown as **Cancel**.

❏ Menu items and dialog boxes are shown as **File-Open**.

❏ Filenames, names of fields, documents or anything else named by the user are shown as *Field name*.

❏ Text which you are instructed to type in yourself is shown as ***Filename***.

❏ Keys on the keyboard are shown as <u>*Ctrl*</u>.

Indicates a tip providing a helpful hint or shortcut method.

Indicates a cautionary note.

Indicates a cross reference.

Entering Text

What you will learn in this unit

This unit assumes that the user is familiar with basic text and page formatting and can create simple documents. The activities in this unit are concerned with proofing a document in order to achieve optimum accuracy and precision of expression.

There are various ways in which the word processor can help to improve the text in a document. Many word processor users are not trained typists and are prone to make errors while keying in their work. Word will check your work as you key it in for both spelling and grammatical errors. Mistakes are shown with a wiggly line underneath them, red for spelling errors and green for grammatical errors. You can instantly revise a mistake by clicking on the marked word or phrase with the right mouse button. This generates a shortcut menu through which you can either choose a revision or tell Word to ignore the word or phrase. Even so it is good practice to read your document to check for spelling and grammatical mistakes before printing the final copy. The word processor cannot proof-read a document, so after checking the spelling and grammar always proof-read your work yourself. If the work would benefit from rewording make use of the thesaurus.

At the end of this unit you will be able to:

❑   Check spelling and grammar.

❑   Use AutoCorrect.

❑   Use the thesaurus.

❑   Find and replace word forms.

Checking spelling and grammar as you work

You will already have noticed Word's ability to check your work as you type. Word underlines spelling mistakes in red and grammatical errors in green. If you find this irritating, you may switch off either or both spelling and grammar checking as you work; use **Tools-Options**, select the **Spelling and Grammar** tab and remove the tick from the 'as you type' check boxes.

Spelling mistakes are often the result of a typing error – such as transposing letters in a word – and these can easily be amended. However, there will be a number of occasions when Word will not recognise a word because it is not in its dictionary and will not make any suggestions for correct spelling.

When a spelling error is identified, point to the word and click the *right* mouse button. This displays a shortcut menu which will suggest alternatives, allow you to **Ignore All** occurrences of the word, add the word to the dictionary or start the spell checker (as described in the next section).

When Word notices that a word has been mspelled it places a wiggly line underneath and you can right-click to get a list of possible correctio...

spelled
misspelled
smelled
spilled
Ignore All
Add
AutoCorrect ▶
Language ▶
ABC Spelling...

Grammatical errors may be due to misplaced apostrophes or commas that have been omitted or they may be due to the sentence structure. Word has a limited set of rules for grammar checking so if the revision suggested is not suitable, you can ignore the sentence and use your own judgement. The illustration below shows the shortcut menu (right mouse button) for a grammatical error.

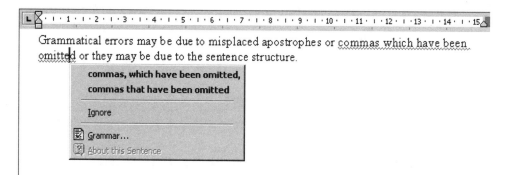

Grammatical errors may be due to misplaced apostrophes or commas which have been omitted or they may be due to the sentence structure.

commas, which have been omitted,
commas that have been omitted
Ignore
Grammar...
About this Sentence

Task 1: Correcting spelling as you work

In this task a document will be created which will be saved as a template. A template is a document that contains standard text, which can be used as the basis for other documents. The letter below is incomplete as it only contains text that would be found in all letters of this type; additional text would be added to customise the document. Templates are considered in more detail in Unit 3.

1. Start a new document and key in the standard letter shown below.

Chelmer Estates
25 High Street
Chelmer
Cheshire
CR1 3QW

Our Ref:

Dear

Re:

We write as promised to confirm our comments with regard to value and saleability of the above mentioned property.

We found the property to comprise

We regard valuation

We enclose our terms and conditions in accordance with the Estate Agents Act 1979, Section 18 as amended with effect from 29th July 1991. If there are any aspects of these that you wish to discuss please do not hesitate to get in touch. We trust you found our comments helpful and look forward to hearing from you.

Yours sincerely

H. D. Jones B.A., E.N.A.E.A
Director
Chelmer Estates

2. Experiment by keying in deliberately misspelt words. Point to these words and click with the right mouse button to see the shortcut menu. Either choose one of the suggestions or the **Ignore All** option; do not add any words to the dictionary or start the **Spell Checker**.

3. Save the document as a template by using **File-Save As** and choosing **Document Template** from the **Save as type** list box. Give the document the name *Value and Saleability*.

Task 2: Correcting grammar as you work

The following piece of text is deliberately incorrect. Key it into a new document exactly as shown on the next page.

1. There are three instances of 'its' that should be 'it's'. However, the grammar checker may not detect them all. Those that are found are signalled with a wiggly green line.

2. There are two other mistakes that neither the spell checker or grammar checker will find. These are 'expect advice' which should read 'expert advice' and 'god news' instead of 'good news'. Correct these.

IMPORTANT QUESTIONS, HONEST ANSWERS TO HELP GET YOU MOVING

Buying or selling a property should be exciting and fun, but its certainly one of the most important decisions you'll ever make.

Its important that, before you make any decisions, you know the facts and seek out the soundest advice, so that you can turn what could be seen as hurdles, into easily managed steps.

Naturally, you'd expect Chelmer Estates to know all of the answers, and to offer you sound, honest and expect advice.

That's precisely why we've introduced an important service for anyone thinking of moving home.

It is called **Budgeting Advice** and the god news is that its absolutely free!

3. The spell checker also identifies 'Chelmer' as an error; the spelling is correct in this case so the 'error' can be ignored.

4. Save the text as a Word document (not as a template), *Budgeting advice*.

Using the spelling and grammar checker

The spelling and grammar checker can be used to check a selection or the whole document. In large documents that are subject to repeated amendment, working on specific selections is more efficient than working through the full document.

If a selection is to be checked, select it first. The spelling and grammar checker can be activated in any of the following ways:

❏ Use **Tools-Spelling and Grammar**.

❏ Click on the ABC button.

❏ Use the shortcut key *F7*.

❏ Choose **Spelling** or **Grammar** from the shortcut menu (right mouse button).

If you have not made a selection, Word will start the spelling and grammar check from the position of the insertion point.

The **Spelling and Grammar** dialog box appears. If you only want to check your document for spelling mistakes and not grammatical errors, then remove the tick from the **Check grammar** check box.

When the spelling and grammar checker comes across a misspelt word it shows it in red in the **Not in Dictionary** box. In the **Suggestions** box the spell checker offers a list of possible corrections.

There are now a number of options available, shown by the buttons:

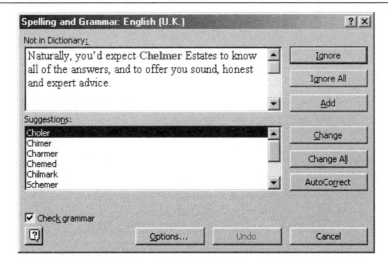

❏ If the correct spelling is highlighted in the **Suggestions** box, click on the **Change** button.

❏ If the correct spelling is in the **Suggestions** box, but is not highlighted, select it and click on the **Change** button.

❏ If you think that the mistake may be repeated throughout the document then use the **Change All** button instead of the **Change** button.

❏ If the word is correct but it is not in the spell checker's dictionary then choose **Ignore** or you may **Add** the word to the dictionary. Consult the Office Assistant for information about adding to or creating your own dictionary. Use **Ignore All** to ignore all occurrences of the word throughout the document.

❏ If the word is a mistake that you commonly make then you may add it to Word's list of AutoCorrect entries by clicking on the **AutoCorrect** button. AutoCorrect is discussed below.

If a selection is not made, the spell checker will check the entire document, and when finished will return to the original place of the insertion point. If you are checking a selection, when that is finished you have the option to carry on and check the whole document.

If you are checking grammar as well as spelling, whenever the checker comes across a grammatical error, the error is shown in the upper box. The title states the type of error.

Words related to the suspected error are displayed in green type. The spelling and grammar checker displays suggested corrections in the **Suggestions** box. The following choices of action are available:

❏ Make a suggested correction.

Select one of the corrections from the **Suggestions** box and click on the **Change** button.

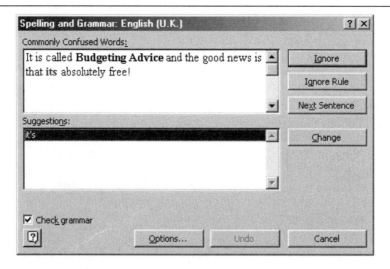

❏ Make your own corrections in the document.

Make the document window active by clicking on it. Edit the sentence and click on the **Resume** button in the dialog box to resume checking the document.

❏ Ignore the questioned word or sentence without making changes.

Click on the **Ignore** button.

❏ Skip the entire sentence.

Click on the **Next Sentence** button to start checking the next sentence.

❏ Customise the grammatical rules used for checking.

Click on the **Options** button. Refer to the Office Assistant for the grammatical rules that are available.

AutoCorrect

You can tell Word about your common typing errors so that, as you type, Word will monitor your typing for these mistakes and automatically correct them. Word maintains a list of common 'mistypes' and their corrections. For example the word 'occurrance' would be corrected as 'occurrence'. If you do not wish Word to make automatic corrections, you can switch off this feature using **Tools-AutoCorrect** and remove the tick from the **Replace text as you type** check box.

You may add mistyped words and their corrections to the AutoCorrect list, either using **Tools-AutoCorrect** or by clicking on the **AutoCorrect** button in the Spelling and Grammar dialog box.

The **AutoCorrect** dialog box also offers the following corrections which you may switch on or off by either ticking the appropriate check box or leaving it blank:

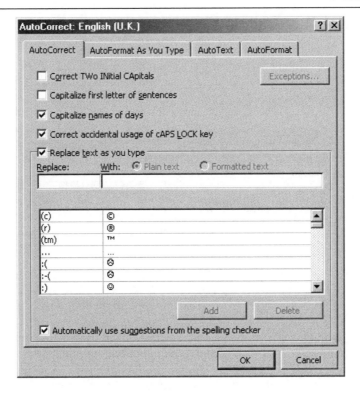

❏ Correction of two capitals at the beginning of a word (this may happen if you type quickly and do not release the *Shift* key soon enough)

❏ Capitalisation of the first word of a sentence

❏ Capitalisation of the names of the days of the week

❏ Correction of typing when *Caps Lock* has been left on and the first word is lower case and the rest upper case (this also switches off *Caps Lock*)

Task 3: Making an AutoCorrect entry

1. Choose **Tools-AutoCorrect** and see that the **Replace text as you type** check box is checked.

2. In the **Replace** box type *usualy* (this is an example of a common mistake).

3. In the **With** box type *usually* (the correct spelling) and click on **Add**. Click on **OK**.

4. In a new document, experiment with misspelling this word. You may add other words that you commonly mistype. Do not save this document.

   Note that if you click on the **AutoCorrect** button in the Spelling and Grammar dialog box Word will add your mistake and the selected change to the list.

Using the Thesaurus

The Thesaurus can be used to add variety and interest to your work: it suggests synonyms and related words. The Thesaurus is used for one word at a time. Place the insertion point in the appropriate word and then choose **Tools-Language-Thesaurus** (shortcut key *Shift+F7*). The Thesaurus dialog box is displayed.

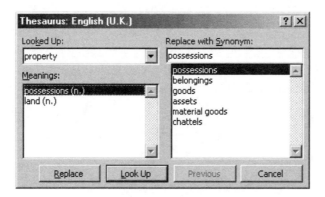

The word that was selected appears in the **Looked Up** box. Underneath this is the **Meanings** box that lists related words and indicates whether these words are nouns or verbs. Next to the **Looked Up** box is a **Replace with Synonym** box that contains a list of synonyms for the selected word. You can replace the selected word with any of the words listed by clicking on one of the alternatives. The new word appears in the text box at the top of the list and clicking on the **Replace** button will put it into the document in place of the original word.

If the list of synonyms is not extensive enough then the Thesaurus can be used to find synonyms for the selected word. To do this, click on one of the synonyms and then on the **Look Up** button. This procedure may be repeated until a suitable synonym is found.

The Thesaurus keeps a list of all the words you have looked up. To return to a previous word open the **Looked Up** list box by clicking on the arrow at the end of the box. Previous words are displayed and the required word can be chosen from the list.

Task 4: Using the Thesaurus

Add the text on the opposite page to the document *Budgeting advice* and save it.

Using the Thesaurus investigate synonyms for the following words: 'mutually', 'programme', 'affordable' and 'aspirations'.

1. Place the insertion point in the word to be investigated.

2. Use **Tools-Language-Thesaurus**.

Here's how Budgeting Advice works for you

Because buying a home is so important, it's equally important that you understand clearly your own financial position.

Our aim is simply to advise you so that you can be certain that the home of your dreams is realistic and affordable now, and in the years to come.

How to get Budgeting Advice working for you

Simply call into or telephone your nearest Chelmer Estates branch and arrange a mutually convenient date and time to meet one of our 'Budgeting Advice' team. You'll find them friendly, helpful and highly knowledgeable.

The initial formal chat will broadly cover your own requirements and analyse your financial situation. If a further meeting is necessary, then a more in-depth financial analysis will take place, to ensure that you can consider all of the mortgage options available.

In addition to this valuable, free service, we can also consider your long term financial planning, and so provide a sound programme that will keep pace with your prospects and your aspirations.

3. Consider whether a replacement should be selected from the list of synonyms.

4. Investigate the effect of 'looking up' a word. Remember that a list of words looked up can be viewed by opening the **Looked Up** list box.

Finding and replacing noun or adjective forms or verb tenses

No doubt you will be familiar with Word's ability to find and replace words. This facility can be used in a more sophisticated way to replace word forms.

❑ You can replace singular and plural noun forms at the same time: for example, replacing 'house' with 'property' and 'houses' with 'properties'.

❑ You can replace all adjective forms: for example, replacing 'worse' with 'better' at the same time as replacing 'worst' with 'best'.

❑ You can replace all tenses of a root verb: for example, replacing 'sell' with 'buy' at the same time as replacing 'sold' with 'bought'.

To find and replace word forms follow this procedure:

1. Choose **Edit-Replace** and in the **Find what** box, type the word to find (for example, 'get') or click the down arrow to select one of the most recent entries.

2. In the **Replace with** box, type the replacement word (for example, 'obtain') or click the down arrow to select one of the most recent entries.

3. Click on **More**, tick the **Find all word forms** check box and click on **Replace** or **Replace All**.

Using **Replace All** choose **Replace** after Word finds each word form allows you to confirm that Word is replacing the correct forms of the words you've specified. You should always be careful with the **Replace All** option, even for an ordinary replace; for example, if you replace 'program' with 'programme' you could produce 'programmeme' where the original word was 'programme'. One way to avoid this is to include a space at the end of both the 'find what' and 'replace with' words.

 Note that you may have to install this version of the **Replace** command from the Office CD before you can use it.

Task 5: Finding and replacing word forms

1. Key in the following text:

Our house advertising is planned in great detail, and designed to gain maximum coverage for your home. We have an excellent reputation for selling houses quickly, so why not come to see us first?

---

2. Using **Edit-Replace** replace all word forms of 'house' with 'property'. Click on **More**, tick the **Find All Word Forms** check box and click on **Replace** to make two replacements.

    Do not save this document.

Printing a Document

What you will learn in this unit

Having created and saved a document it is usual to print it. The activities in this unit are concerned with investigating the different print options available and also the printing of document statistics. Elements of document and file management are also considered.

At the end of this unit you will be able to:

❑ Select a printer (if you have a choice of printers or fax), investigate printer properties and cancel a print job.

❑ Control page margins and use the 'Shrink to Fit' option.

❑ Print selected parts of a document, collate multiple copies and print 'double sided' (i.e. on both sides of the paper).

❑ Print on different sizes of paper and envelopes.

What you need

To complete this unit you will need:

❑ The document file *Budgeting advice* created in Unit 1

Printing options

Word provides several options for the way in which a document is printed.

Selecting a printer

If you are using a standalone machine then it is likely that you will have a single dedicated printer connected to your computer and normally you will not need to think about selecting a printer. However, if you have a fax/modem installed on your computer you can print directly to this in the same way as you would print to a printer.

If you are using a network then you may have the choice of different printers for different applications. For example, you may use a laser printer for high quality, high volume, high speed printouts or a colour printer for smaller, low volume, specialised jobs. You may also be able to 'print' to a fax/modem.

To select a printer:

1. Proof and save the document you intend to print or fax.

2. Choose **File-Print** and in the **Printer** section, open the **Name** drop-down list. This will display the list of printers and fax systems that are available. If you are using a portable printer then check you have connected it to your machine and it is loaded with paper and ready before trying to print to it.

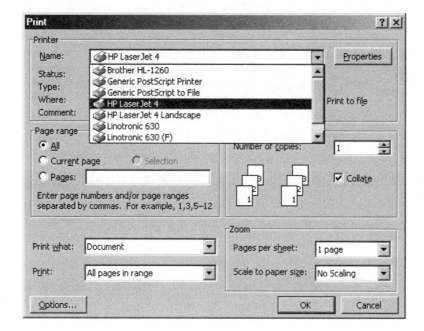

3. Select the required printer or fax. Remember that changing printer can cause slight layout differences so preview the document before printing. Make any changes as necessary. Use **File-Print** and click on **OK** or click on the 🖨 button in the toolbar.

4. If you are faxing the document then your fax application will start and you should select the recipient from your address list or key in their details and then send the fax.

Investigating the printer's properties

Choose **File-Print** and click on the **Properties** button. The properties that you see will be dependent on the printer but you are likely to be able to control print quality, paper feed and orientation, and collation of printed output.

Task 1: Printing a document

1. Open the document *Budgeting advice*, add the text below and save it.

Make your next move with real peace of mind

On approval of your completed financial analysis, we will present you with your Personal Home Buying Certificate. This will give you the peace of mind that, when you are making an offer on a property, you'll know the level of mortgage you can afford.

It's nice to know that when you're ready to move, Budgeting Advice will have made it possible for you to move quickly. With all discussions out of the way, your mortgage application will be made easier, whether you buy from Chelmer Estates or not.

With Budgeting Advice, you need never take chances. Instead you'll enjoy the complete peace of mind that comes with friendly, expert and professional – Chelmer – advice.

Call in and see us soon.

---

2. Choose **File-Print** and click on the **Properties** button. Investigate the printer properties. If you have a choice of printers then you may wish to select one of these from the **Name** drop-down list and investigate its properties.

3. Print the document to a printer connected to your computer.

Background printing

You can print in background mode or not depending on the priority you wish to attach to printing. When background printing is on, you can continue to work in Word while you print. Background printing uses additional system memory, slowing the printing process. To speed up printing, switch off background printing (you will not be able to continue to work in Word until the print job has been sent). To turn background printing on or off:

1. Choose **Tools-Options**, and then click on the **Print** tab.

2. Under the **Printing** options, tick the **Background printing** check box to switch on; remove the tick to switch off.

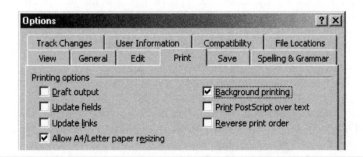

Cancelling a print job

To cancel a print job:

❏ If background printing is turned off, click on **Cancel** or press _Esc_.

❏ If background printing is turned on, double-click the printer icon on the status bar. This will display the print job queue. You can select the print job and cancel it by pressing _Delete_.

If you're printing a short document and background printing is turned on, the printer icon may not appear on the status bar long enough for you to click it to cancel printing.

Page Setup

Page Setup, on the **File** menu, allows you to set a number of parameters that specify how the document will be displayed on the page. Four main options are available:

❏ Margins

❏ Paper Size

❏ Paper Source

❏ Layout

Each of these has a separate dialog box that is displayed when the appropriate tab is clicked. Many of the options in these dialog boxes are self-explanatory and the preview helps to indicate the effect of modifications.

Controlling page margins

Under the **Margins** tab of **Page Setup**, there are two important characteristics:

❏ The part of the document to which the settings are to be applied

❏ Whether facing pages need to be set with mirrored margins, as in a book, to allow for binding

Margins can be adjusted in Page Layout view or Print Preview. Dragging the margin boundary on the ruler will change the margins in a section or an entire document.

To display the measurements of the text area and the margins, hold down the _Alt_ key as you drag the boundary.

If you plan to bind a document in any way (including the use of a ring binder), defining a size for a gutter margin will add extra space to the inside margin. To create a gutter margin use **File-Page Setup**, choose the **Margins** tab and then set a width for your gutter margin.

You may wish to print a document on both sides of the paper, as in a book; this gives you left and right-handed pages. To set margins on facing pages to mirror one another (i.e. so that inside and outside margins have the same width), use **File-Page Setup**, choose the **Margins** tab and tick the **Mirror margins** check box. You may adjust the widths of the inside and outside margins as necessary.

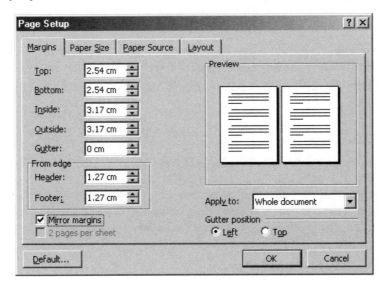

Shrink to fit

When you preview a document you may find that a small amount of text appears on the last page. To prevent this you may be able to reduce the number of pages by clicking on the ![shrink to fit icon] (**Shrink to Fit**) button in Print Preview. This feature works best with documents that contain only a few pages, such as letters and memos. In order to shrink the document, Word decreases the font size of each font used in the document.

If you do not like the result of the shrink-to-fit operation you can use **Edit-Undo Shrink to Fit**. However, after you save the document and close it, there is no quick way to restore the original font size.

Printing selected parts of a document

It is not necessary to print a whole document, particularly if it is more than one page long. Through the Print dialog box a selected set of pages, the current page or a selection may be printed.

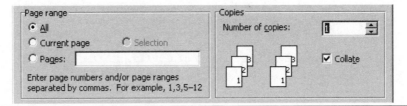

Collating multiple copies

If you are printing more than one copy of a document that is more than one page long, you can tick the **Collate** check box so that the documents will be printed in proper binding order.

Printing in reverse order

Some printers produce pages face down, so that they end up in the correct order. With others, however, the first page is at the bottom and the last page at the top in the printer output tray. In these cases, the order of printing may be reversed. To do this:

1. Choose **Tools-Options** and select the **Print** tab.

2. Under **Printing Options**, tick the **Reverse print order** check box.

Word prints the document in reverse order, beginning with the last page. You should use this option when printing multiple collated copies that are to be bound. If you are printing an envelope don't select this option.

Printing on different sizes of paper

In the UK the standard size of paper used for printing is A4. However, for some documents you may wish to use an alternative size. You can choose any size but your printer will ultimately limit the width of paper that you can print on.

To change the paper size use **File-Page Setup** and select the **Paper Size** tab. Open the **Paper Size** drop-down list and select the size of paper required. You may also change the orientation of the paper. If your paper is not a standard size then choose **Custom Size** and enter the size of the paper into the **Width** and **Height** boxes.

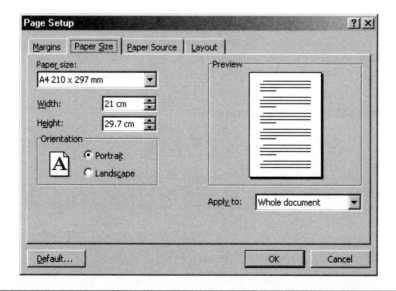

Printing an address on an envelope

If you only want to print an occasional envelope use the method described below. If you print many envelopes on a regular basis then you should use mail merge (see *Word 2000 Basic Skills* or consult the on-line help).

To print on an envelope, proceed as follows:

1. Choose **Tools-Envelopes and Labels** and select the **Envelopes** tab as illustrated.

2. Enter the address information. To format the address, select the address text, click the right mouse button and choose **Font** on the shortcut menu. Apply the required formatting.

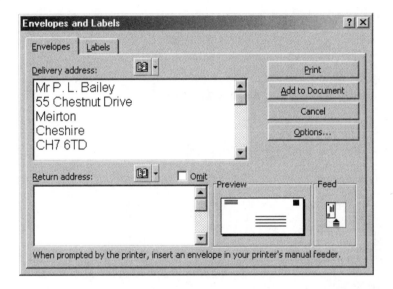

3. To select an envelope size, the type of paper feed and other options, click on the **Options** button.

4. To print the envelope, insert the envelope in the printer as shown in the **Feed** box and click on the **Print** button.

 Warning Do not load normal envelopes into a laser printer. The heat generated by the printing process will affect the gum on the envelope, which may then damage the printer.

To add the envelope as a separate section at the beginning of the document, click on the **Add to Document** button. You can print the envelope when you print the document.

To change an existing envelope that's already a section in a document, click on the envelope text, select **Tools-Envelopes and Labels** and click on the **Change Document** button.

You can create a default return address that appears on all the envelopes you print, or you can include a logo or other graphic images with your return address.

Change the size of an envelope

To change the size of the envelope being printed:

1. Choose **Tools-Envelopes and Labels** and select the **Envelopes** tab.

2. Click on the **Options** button and choose the **Envelope Options** tab.

3. Open the drop-down **Envelope size** box and select the required envelope size. If the size you want is not listed, choose **Custom size** and then enter the dimensions of your envelope.

Task 2: Adding an address to a document

Our ref: SJC/341/HDJ/CHELMER OFFICE

28 October 2001

Mr P. L. Bailey
55 Chestnut Drive
Meirton
Cheshire
CR7 6TD

Dear Mr Bailey

Re: 55 Chestnut Drive, Meirton, Cheshire.

We have pleasure in confirming the proposed sale of the above property to Ms A. McAllister for the agreed sum of £46,000 subject to contract.

We have passed the relevant information to your solicitor who will proceed with the necessary contractual arrangements and keep us advised of developments.

If there is any further information that you require, please do not hesitate to contact us.

Yours sincerely

H. D. Jones B.A., F.N.A.E.A
Director
CHELMER ESTATES

In this task a simple letter is created and the address will be added so that both letter and envelope may be printed.

1. Create the letter above and save it as *Bailey P sale confirmation*.

2. Choose **Tools-Envelopes and Labels**, and select the **Envelopes** tab. The address used on the letter should already appear in the **Delivery address** box. Note that you can amend this address if required.

3. If you wish to specify the envelope size, click on **Options** and choose the required size. Click on **OK**.

4. Click on the **Add to Document** button. The address is added to the document as a separate section (as shown below).

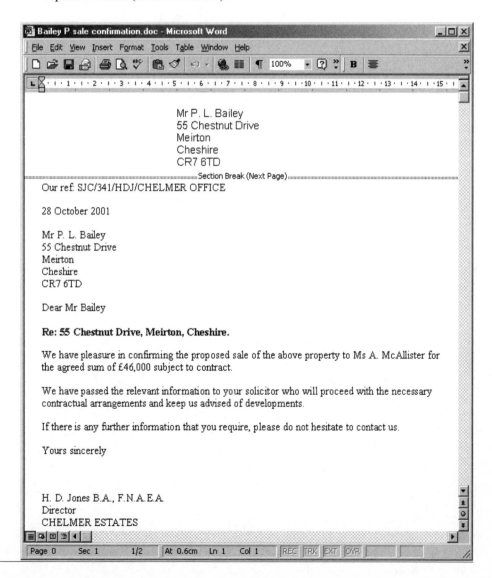

5.   Save and close the document.

Using Templates

What you will learn in this unit

The activities described in this unit are aimed at reducing the amount of keying that might be performed in producing a document, by using templates and the AutoText facility. In business there are many occasions where standard documents – such as letters, memos, faxes, reports, invoices and delivery notes – are produced repeatedly. Often most features such as the firm's address, logo, text font and layout of boxes and lines are consistent across a set of documents. Using a template to hold such features is the best way to maintain consistency and to establish a corporate identity.

In Unit 1 Task 1 a very simple and plain standard letter template was created simply by typing the standard elements of a letter and saving them as a template. By basing other documents on this template only the more specific details need be added to complete the document. This unit looks at further template options.

AutoText allows you to assign a simple key combination to a long word or phrase. When the assigned key combination is used the word or phrase will appear in the document. AutoText is not limited to text entries; other objects such as graphics may also be made into AutoText entries.

At the end of this unit you will be able to:

- ❏ Use a template.
- ❏ Create a template based on an existing template.
- ❏ Modify a template.
- ❏ Create AutoText entries.
- ❏ Print AutoText entries.

What you need

To complete this unit you will need:

- ❏ The template file *Value and Saleability* created in Unit 1

Task 1: Using a template

1. Use **File-New-More Word Templates** and select the *Value and Saleability* template, created in Unit 1, from the **General** tab.

2. Complete the letter as follows. Use **Insert-Date and Time** to add the date. Save the letter as *Pattison D V&S* and print it.

Chelmer Estates
25 High Street
Chelmer
Cheshire
CR1 3QW

Our Ref: SJC/972/HDJ/CRELMER OFFICE

20 October 2001

Mrs D. Pattison
34 Cedar Close
Chelmer
Cheshire
CR5 7RY

Dear Mrs Pattison

Re: 34 Cedar Close, Chelmer

We write as promised to confirm our comments with regard to value and saleability of the above mentioned property.

We found the property to comprise a modem semi-detached dwelling.

We regard valuation as lying reasonably in the region of £75,000 and would suggest an initial asking price of £78,000 subject to contract, as a test of market reaction.

We enclose our terms and conditions in accordance with the Estate Agents Act 1979, Section 18 as amended with effect from 29th July 1991. If there are any aspects of these that you wish to discuss please do not hesitate to get in touch. We trust you found our comments helpful and look forward to hearing from you.

Yours sincerely

H. D. Jones B.A., E.N.A.E.A
Director
Chelmer Estates

Creating templates

A template is a predefined format for a document. A template can be used to define not only standard text but also aspects such as the font, borders, page size and orientation. Once a template has been created it can be recalled and used to produce the required document.

Word comes with many predefined templates that you can use to create documents such as letters and memos. To create most documents the 'normal document' template, *Normal.dot*, is used. This is the template that you have been using to create your documents. If a document is started using **File-New-More Word Templates** then a dialog box containing the names of the templates appears: these are grouped by type, which you select by clicking on the appropriate tab. By choosing **General** you can select the Normal template file. Template files have the extension *.dot* and are stored in a special subdirectory.

Word provides other template files, such as a standard letter and memo, and it is possible to customise these.

You may base a new template on an existing template:

1. Choose **File-New-More Word Templates**. Select a template that is similar to the one you want to create, click on **Template** under **Create New** and then click on **OK**.

2. Choose **File-Save As**. In the **Save as type** list, the **Document Template (*.dot)** file type is already be selected.

3. Word proposes the *Templates* folder in the **Save in** box. To save the template so that it will appear on a tab other than **General**, create a folder by clicking on the 🗁 (**Create New Folder**) button and open that folder.

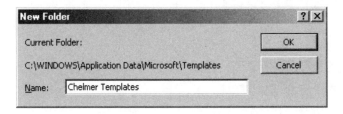

4. In the **File Name** box, type a name for the new template and then click on **Save**.

5. In the new template, add the text and graphics you want to appear in all new documents that are based on the template, and delete any items you do not want to appear.

6. Make the changes you want to the margin settings, page size and orientation, styles, and other formats.

7. Choose **File-Save** and close the template.

Task 2: Creating a memo template based on an existing template

This is the easiest way to create a template, particularly if your template is going to be very similar in layout to one of the ones that comes with Word.

1. Choose **File-New-More Word Templates** and click on the **Memos** tab. Select the *Contemporary Memo* template, under **Create New** choose the **Template** option, and click on **OK**.

2. Choose **File-Save As**. Click on the ⊡ (**Create New Folder**) button and create a folder called *Chelmer Templates*.

3. In the **File Name** box, type **Chelmer Estates Memo** and then click on **Save**.

4. Customise the memo by making some formatting changes to the font of the text and by removing the instructions from the body of the memo. Delete the background graphics. (Most of these are in the header and footer; display them with **View-Header and Footer**, click on them and press *Delete*.)

5. Add a text box (from the Drawing toolbar) containing the text *Chelmer Estates*. Save and close.

---

chelmer
estates

Memorandum

To: [Click **here** and type name]

CC: [Click **here** and type name]

From: [Click **here** and type name]

Date: 20/09/2001

Re: [Click **here** and type subject]

Task 3: Modifying a customised template

1. Choose **File-Open** and select **Document Template** in the **Files of type** box.

2. Open the *Chelmer Templates* subfolder. (To find the folder, select **Tools-Options** and click on the **File Locations** tab. The parent folder is specified by the *User templates* item and can be viewed by clicking on the **Modify** button. You can change this location if you wish, but remember to move any existing templates if you do so.) Select *Chelmer Estates Memo*.

3. Make another formatting change and save and close the template document.

---

4. Use this template to create the following memo. Save as *Pattison Memo*.

**chelmer
estates**

Memorandum

To: Jane Fellows

cc:

From: Peter Smith

Date: 20/10/2001

Re: Pattison, 34 Cedar Close, Chelmer

Our client has contacted me regarding the sale of her property and has asked us to proceed with the sale, so please could you arrange for the property to be photographed.

Using fields

In the memo above, the date is added to the template using **Insert-Date and Time**, selecting a suitable format and ticking the **Update Automatically** check box. There are many types of fields that can be added to a document; those which are most useful to standard letters and templates are the document filename, the author and perhaps the template that was used to create the document. These fields would usually be added to the document footer, often using a small type size, and provide useful traceability for the document. Unit 4 shows you how to add a field to a document header or footer.

Creating AutoText entries

Word uses AutoText to save repeated keying of the same text. Some documents contain text (and/or graphics) which is repeated many times. For example, a company name, address or logo may appear several times in one document or may be required in many documents. By defining the name, address or logo as an AutoText entry it may be recalled at any point in any document with a simple keying action. Take a simple example: the text *Yours sincerely* appears at the end of many business letters. If many letters are to be typed then defining this as an AutoText entry would help to save time keying.

Word maintains a list of AutoText entries that you can add to or delete from. An AutoText entry may be text, graphics or a mixture of both text and graphics. You can save text or graphics that you use frequently as an AutoText entry. Then you can easily insert the text or graphics into a document with a simple keying action, rather than retyping or using copy and paste.

Making an AutoText entry

First type in the text (e.g. *Chelmer Estates*) that you intend to make into an AutoText entry. Check that spelling is correct and select the text. If you wish to store the paragraph formatting as part of the AutoText entry then include the paragraph mark in the selection. Choose **Insert-AutoText-AutoText**, click on **AutoText** and the AutoCorrect dialog box appears.

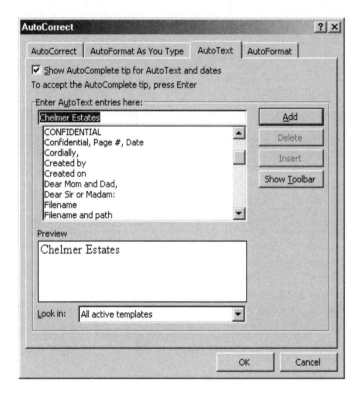

In the **Enter AutoText entries here** box type a name for the AutoText entry: in this example, *c* for Chelmer Estates. Then click on the **Add** button.

Alternatively use **Insert-AutoText-New**, type in a name for the AutoText and click on **OK**.

Using an AutoText entry

The simplest method of using an AutoText entry is to type the AutoText name followed immediately by *F3* (function key 3): i.e. typing *c* and pressing *F3* would produce the text *Chelmer Estates*.

Alternatively, if you forget your AutoText names, then use **Insert-AutoText-AutoText**. The dialog box lists your previously defined AutoText entries. Type or select the AutoText name you wish to use and click on the **Insert** button.

AutoText prompts

You may have noticed that as you begin to type some words – for example, days of the week – Word prompts you with the completed word or phrase. This is another way in which AutoText works. If, instead of using *c* as the AutoText name for *Chelmer Estates*, the full text was used as the name then, as you began to type 'Chelmer', you would be prompted with the full text. You may have both names defined so that you can either use *c+F3* or expect to be prompted each time you type 'Chelmer'.

Depending on the frequency with which you would use AutoText as a shortcut you would choose to use either an AutoText entry or an AutoText prompt. For a shortcut that you frequently use an AutoText entry is probably preferable; choose an AutoText name for the entry that you can easily remember (one or more letters).

Task 4: Creating and using AutoText entries

Open a new document and try setting up and using AutoText entries.

1. Type out the AutoText entry in full, e.g. *Yours faithfully*.

2. Select this text, use **Insert-AutoText-New**, accept *Yours faithfully* as the name for the AutoText entry and click on **OK**.

3. Start typing **Yours faithfully** and you should be prompted when you reach the 'f' of 'faithfully'; press *Enter* to accept the prompt.

4. Now create shortcut AutoText entries as follows:

AutoText name	AutoText entry
ys	Yours sincerely
yf	Yours faithfully
ms	Microsoft Word

In each case, type out the AutoText entry in full, e.g. *Yours sincerely*. Select the new text. Use **Insert-AutoText-AutoText** and in the **Enter AutoText entries here** box type the AutoText name, e.g. *ys*.

5. Click on **Add**. Move the insertion point to a place where the AutoText entry is to appear.

6. Type the AutoText name (e.g. *ys*) and press *F3*.

Experiment with creating other AutoText entries. Do not save this document.

Task 5: Assigning clipart to an AutoText entry

1. Start a new document. Add clipart to the document by using **Insert-Picture-Clip Art**. Choose a suitable item of clipart. Adjust the size of the clipart by dragging a corner sizing handle to make it smaller.

2. While it is selected choose **Insert-AutoText-New** and in the **Create AutoText** box type the AutoText name. Click on **OK**.

3. Move the insertion point to a place where the AutoText graphic is to appear.

4. Type the AutoText name and press *F3*.

Do not save this document. However, the AutoText entry will be available to other documents. You may delete the AutoText entry using the steps below.

Deleting AutoText entries

To remove an AutoText entry:

1. Choose **Insert-AutoText-AutoText**. Scroll through the list of AutoText entries until you find the entry you wish to delete.

2. Highlight the entry, click on **Delete** and **OK**.

Printing AutoText entries

AutoText entries can be printed by selecting **AutoText entries** from the **Print what** list box in the Print dialog box.

Page Layout

What you will learn in this unit

In this unit the activities concentrate on word processing features that are applicable to documents of more than one page. At the end of this unit you will be able to:

❑ Format paragraphs.

❑ Control page breaks.

❑ Number pages.

❑ Add headers and footers.

❑ Add footnotes and endnotes.

For most long documents it is useful to know how to add headers, footers and page numbers and to be able to control page breaks.

You may be working on a document that will eventually be many pages long or you may wish to combine several documents, or parts of them, into one larger one.

What you need

To complete this unit you will need:

❑ The document file *Budgeting advice* created in Unit 1 and amended in Unit 2

❑ The document file *Chelmer Estates Memo* created in Unit 3

Paragraph formatting

You will be very unlikely to find printed matter where the text is not divided into paragraphs, which are easily identifiable. Paragraphs are either denoted by an indent (first line set in slightly from the left margin) or by the use of space between paragraphs. The second method is more common; the first method is generally used where text is arranged in columns. Inexperienced users of word processors tend to separate paragraphs with a blank line. More professionally, instead of pressing *Enter* to create a blank line between paragraphs Word allows you to define the amount of space before and after a paragraph.

Use **Format-Paragraph** to display the Paragraph dialog box and in the **Spacing** section the values in the **Before** and **After** boxes can be adjusted. Spacing is altered in increments of six points, which can be considered to be half a line. You will usually add the space after the paragraph, rather than before.

Other paragraphs may require different spacing – for example headings or tables – and this can be easily adjusted from the Paragraph dialog box.

Task 1: Controlling space between paragraphs

This task experiments with altering the spacing between paragraphs. Open the document *Budgeting advice*.

1. If you have blank lines in between paragraphs, remove them. To help you do this you can display the paragraph marks by clicking on the ¶ icon.

2. Mark the whole document. Choose **Format-Paragraph** and set the **Spacing After** to 6 points (half a line).

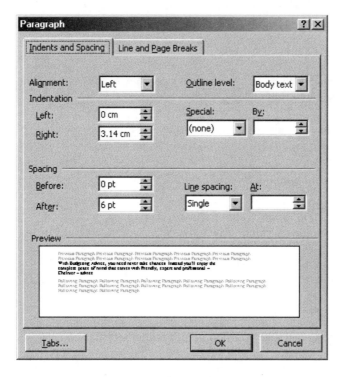

3. Position the insertion point in the first paragraph (the main heading). Choose **Format-Paragraph** and set the **Spacing After** to 12 points (one line).

4. Position the insertion point in first sub-heading. Choose **Format-Paragraph** and set the **Spacing Before** to 12 points (one line). Note that the spacing after the paragraph above now has no effect.

5. Use the Format Painter to copy this spacing to the other sub-headings. Save the changes.

Experiment with setting the line spacing before and after the paragraphs in this document.

Page breaks

As the document being created gets larger, Word automatically inserts a page break at the end of each page. Automatic page breaks are called *soft* breaks and are shown in Normal view as a dotted line. As the document is edited and revised Word repositions the page breaks accordingly. This is known as *repagination*. Repagination occurs whenever you pause during keying. To alter the way in which page breaks occur, then manual or *hard* breaks can be inserted.

Adding or removing page breaks

To add a hard page break:

1. Position the insertion point at the place where the page break is to occur.

2. Either use **Insert-Break** and select **Page Break** from the Break dialog box or press *Ctrl+Enter* simultaneously.

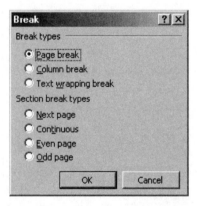

In Normal view a dotted line appears at the point of the hard page break, with the words *Page Break* in the middle of the line.

A hard page break may be selected in the same way as selecting a line of text, i.e. by positioning the mouse pointer in the left edge of the screen, level with the page break and clicking. Once selected the page break can be removed. It is not possible to remove *soft* page breaks; these can be controlled either by inserting hard page breaks or with paragraph formatting. If possible it is best to avoid hard page breaks in a long document as they need to be revised manually whenever the document is revised.

Controlling page breaks using paragraph formatting

Page breaks are controlled through the pagination section of the **Line and Page Breaks** tab in the **Format-Paragraph** dialog box. There are three types of formatting available:

❑ **Keep Lines Together**: use this to prevent a page break within a paragraph. (Word normally exercises Widow and Orphan control if the **Widow/Orphan Control** box is checked; that is to say, it will prevent widows and orphans from occurring. A *widow* is a single line at the beginning of a paragraph left at the bottom of a page and an *orphan* is a single line at the end of a paragraph at the top of a page.)

❑ **Keep with Next**: use this to prevent a page break occurring between the paragraph and the following one: for example, to keep a sub-heading with its following paragraph or to keep the lines of a table together.

❑ **Page Break Before**: a page break is inserted before the paragraph. If each chapter of your document is to appear on a new page, then format the chapter heading style with **Page Break Before** by clicking in the appropriate check box. To remove this page break for a particular heading the formatting must be removed from the paragraph.

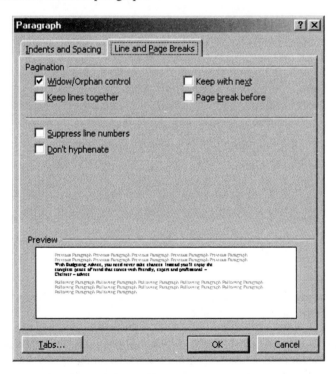

By making use of these formatting options the need for hard pages breaks to be inserted in a long document can be eliminated. When the document is altered the page breaks will follow the rules applied in the paragraph formatting and consequently should occur in sensible places.

Page numbering

There are two methods of inserting page numbers:

❑ Page numbering using **Insert-Page Numbers**. Page numbers may be placed at the bottom or top of the page. The alignment of the number can be chosen and whether or not all pages are to be numbered except the first. Remove the tick from the **Show Number on First Page** box to omit the number from the first page; this is useful for documents that have a title page as the first page.

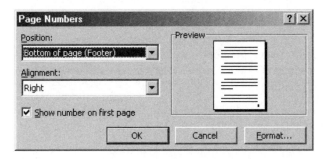

❑ Page numbering as part of a header or footer (see *Headers and Footers* below).

Task 2: Page numbering

Apply page numbering to the document *Budgeting advice*:

1. Use **Insert-Page Numbers** to add page numbers to the document.

2. Check that **Position: Bottom of Page (Footer)** and **Alignment: Centre** are selected.

3. Tick the **Show Number on First Page** check box. Click on **OK**.

4. Change to Page Layout view. The page numbers should be visible at the bottom of each page.

5. Use **File-Print Preview** to see the effect. If the footer does not show properly, this may be due to the printer you have installed. Some printers are not able to print right to the bottom of the paper. Use **File-Page Setup-Margins**, increase the size in the **Footer** box and preview again.

6. Save and close the document.

Headers and footers

A header is text or graphics that appears at the top of every page. A footer appears at the bottom of every page. These are useful in long documents as they can be used to indicate, for example, the chapter or section title. In business documents they may contain a reference number or company logo. If the work is a report, a header or footer could be used to put the author's name or the company name and logo on each page. Word prints headers in the top margin and footers in the bottom margin.

As well as being able to add headers and footers that are the same on every page, Word also offers a number of other choices:

❏ If the document is to be printed on both sides of the paper then headers and footers can be set up so that *even numbered* pages have one header and *odd numbered* pages have a different one.

❏ If the first page of the document is different from the rest of the document – for example, it is a title page – then headers and footers can be set so that they are *different on the first page*.

❏ If the document is divided into sections then different headers and footers can be applied to *each section*.

Adding or removing a header or footer

To add a header or a footer to your document, use **View-Header and Footer**. The document switches to Page Layout view with the text of each page shown in grey (or lighter than normal). A Header and Footer toolbar appears.

Headers and footers have preset tabs: there is a centre tab in the middle of the page and a right tab at the right edge of the page. By using the preset tabs, the headers or footers will be consistent through the document. Select a suitable font for your header or footer and tab across to the position required and type in the text. Using the buttons, as described below, enter text for headers and footers as required and when finished click on **Close**.

Icons and buttons in the Header and Footer toolbar

The first button on the header and footer tool bar allows you to insert AutoText. The next set of three buttons are:

❏ Insert page number

❏ Insert number of pages

❏ Format page number

The next two buttons are:

❏ Insert date

❏ Insert time

To put the date, time, page number or number of pages into a header or footer, position the insertion point and then click on the appropriate icon.

The next two buttons are **Page Setup** and **Show/Hide Document Text**. Clicking on **Page Setup** displays the Page Setup dialog box. Clicking on **Show/Hide Document Text** toggles between showing or hiding the document.

The next button is the **Same as Previous** button. Click on this button if the header or footer is to be different from the header or footer in the previous section.

The first button of the final group of three allows you to switch between the header and footer. The next two buttons allow forward and backward movement between different headers or footers. There will only be different headers and footers if **Different First Page** or **Different Odd and Even Pages** have been selected in Page Setup or there are different sections in the document.

When the text for the header or footer has been typed in, click on the button to return to the document text body.

Before printing it is a good idea to preview the document; headers and footers can be positioned by choosing **File-Page Setup** and defining their required position in the **From Edge** section of the Page Setup-Margins dialog box.

Page numbering in headers or footers

By clicking on the **Format Page Number** button in the Header and Footer toolbar or using **Insert-Page Numbers** and clicking on the **Format** button, page numbering can be controlled. The Page Number Format dialog box is displayed.

The format of page numbering may be chosen from the **Format Page Number** box, i.e. Arabic or Roman numerals or alphabetic sequencing. This can be done by opening the **Format Page Number** list box.

It is also possible to alter the number at which page numbering starts. This can be useful if the document is long and is stored in several files. The start page number of the second and subsequent files may be altered accordingly. You can also change the first page number when editing by choosing **Insert-Page Numbers**, clicking on **Format**, then on **Start At** and typing in the start page number and clicking on **OK** and **Close**.

Different formats of page numbering may be used in different sections of a document, for example, a preface may use Roman numerals and the following sections may use Arabic numerals.

Editing or removing existing headers and footers

To remove or edit an existing header or footer:

1. Use **View-Header and Footer** and display either the header or footer using the 🔁 (**Switch Between Header and Footer**) button.

2. Edit the text in the header or footer in the normal fashion. Text may be pasted into the header or footer, or copied from it. To remove the header/footer simply delete all the text.

3. Click on **Close**.

Headers and footers that are different on the first page

It is useful to set headers and footers to be different on the first page to prevent a header appearing on the first page. As there is usually a title on the first page then a header does not look right. However, the same footer could be used by making the first footer identical to the main footer.

1. Choose **View-Header and Footer** and click on the 📖 (**Page Setup**) button.

2. In the **Layout** tab, click in the **Different First Page** check box. Click on **OK**. This will create a First Header and a First Footer as well as the normal Header and Footer. The text in a First Header may be different from the main Header and the text in a First Footer may be different from the Footer.

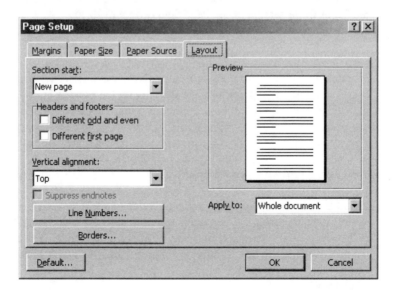

3. Use 🔁 (**Switch Between Header and Footer**), 🔁 (**Show Next**) and 🔁 (**Show Previous**) buttons to navigate to the header or footer required. Key in

the text. To make the main Footer the same as the First Footer, move to the Footer and click on 🔳 (**Same as Previous**).

4. Click on **Close**.

Odd and even headers and footers

Odd and even headers and footers are used when the finished document will be printed, like a book or leaflet, on both sides of the paper. In a book, left-hand pages are even numbered and right-hand pages are odd numbered. A header or footer can be defined so that it reads across from an even to an odd page. Different information about the document can appear on odd and even pages: for example, chapter title on even pages and section title on odd pages. To achieve this:

1. Choose **View-Header and Footer** and click on the 🔳 (**Page Setup**) button.

2. Click on the **Different Odd and Even Pages** check box. This will create an Even Header, Odd Header, Even Footer and Odd Footer. The text in the even header may be different from the odd header and the text in an even footer may be different from the odd footer.

3. Use 🔳 (**Switch Between Header and Footer**), 🔳 (**Show Next**) and 🔳 (**Show Previous**) to navigate to the header or footer required. Key in the text.

4. Click on **Close**.

Note that the odd and even headers/footers option may be used in conjunction with the different first page option.

Task 3: Exploring header and footer options

This task adds some headers and footers to the *Budgeting Advice* document, saving it with a new name.

1. Open the document *Budgeting Advice* and to simulate a long document edit it to start each sub-heading on a new page. To do this select, each heading in turn and use **Format-Paragraph**, select the **Line and Page Breaks** tab and tick the **Page break before** check box. You should end up with four pages. Save the document as *Headers and Footers*.

2. Using **View-Header and Footer**, add the text *Chelmer Estates* to the header and position it on the right.

3. Click on 🔳 (**Switch Between Header and Footer**). Delete the existing page number by clicking on it. clicking on its shaded border and pressing *Delete*.

4. To the centre of the footer add the text *Page* followed by a space, click on the **Insert Page Number** button, add a space, add the text *of* followed by a space and

click on the **Insert Number of Pages** button. Add a top border to the footer using **Format-Borders and Shading**.

5. Save and view the result in Page Layout view; it is also useful to view in Print Preview. If you don't see the footers in Print Preview this may be due to the type of printer you have installed. To remedy this use **File-Page Setup** and increase the measurement specified in the **Footer** part of the **From Edge** section.

6. As a header may look out of place on the first page, the headers and footers on the first page will be made different. Choose **View-Header and Footer**, click on the ▣ (**Page Setup**) button and tick the **Different First Page** check box under the **Layout** tab, then click on **OK**.

7. Leave the first header blank. Switch to the footer and click on the ▣ (**Show Next**) button to display the main Footer text. Select and copy this, use ▣ (**Show Previous**) and paste into the First Footer. Save and view the result.

8. Finally, assume that this document will be printed double-sided. Choose **View-Header and Footer** and click on the ▣ (**Page Setup**) button. Tick the **Different Odd and Even** check box under the **Layout** tab (leave the **Different First Page** check box ticked).

9. View the header and use ▣ (**Show Next**) to move to the Even Header. Add the date using the **Insert Date** button at the left of the header. Try adding a bottom border to this header. Using ▣ move to the odd header, which should still read *Chelmer Estates*, and apply the same bordering as for the even header.

10. Move to the footer. Display the Odd Footer and move the page number to the right-hand side. Copy this and using ▣ (**Show Previous**) paste the text into the Even Footer (you may need to remove an extra paragraph mark). Delete the tabs so that the text is on the left. Display the First Footer and move the page number to the right. Add a top border to all the footers/

11. View the result, you should see headers and footers on the left for even pages and on the right for odd pages. Save the document. If you wish you can experiment further with headers and footers. Shading as well as bordering can be used to good effect in headers and footers.

Using fields in headers and footers

If you add a page number, date or time to a header or footer you are adding a field. Fields are usually highlighted in grey to distinguish them from ordinary text. If you wish to delete a field you will notice that your first deletion action will select the field and the second deletion action will delete it.

Fields other than those available on the Header and Footer toolbar may be inserted into a header and footer, in exactly the same way as they could be inserted into the document text. Fields which may be useful to add to headers and footers include the document filename, author and title.

To add a field:

1. Display the header or footer into which the field is to go and position the insertion point there.

2. Choose **Insert-Field**; the Field dialog box is displayed.

3. Select the field category from the **Categories** box and the field from the **Field names** box. Click on **OK**.

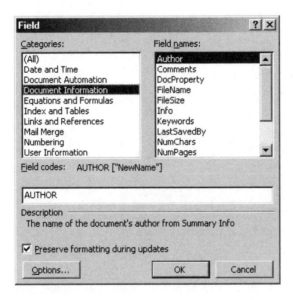

Task 4: Adding a field to a header

1. Open the template *Chelmer Estates Memo* by choosing **File-New-More Word Templates,** clicking on the *Chelmer Templates* tab and double-clicking on the memo icon.

2. Choose **View-Header and Footer**. Click on ▣ (**Page Setup**) and you will see **Different first page** ticked. Display the First Page Header.

3. Using **Insert-Field**, add the filename to the document header. Save the template in the *Chelmer Templates* folder.

4. Open the document *Headers and Footers* and display the First Footer. Using **Insert-Field**, select **Document Information** and choose **Author** to add the writer's name to this footer. Save the document.

Footnotes and endnotes

Footnotes and endnotes are notes of reference, explanation or comment. A word in the main text can be marked with a footnote or endnote reference mark (usually a number). Footnotes are found at the bottom of the page while endnotes are at the end of the document. Word allows footnotes and endnotes of any length to be added to a document. Text used in a footnote can be formatted just as any other text.

To add a footnote or endnote:

1. In Normal view, first position the insertion point at the end of the word that the footnote or endnote is to refer to.

2. Select **Insert-Footnote**; the Footnote and Endnote dialog box appears.

3. Click on **OK** and a footnote pane appears. A reference mark is positioned in the document at the position of the insertion point.

4. Key in the text. The insertion point is ready positioned following the reference mark.

5. Click on **Close**.

As footnotes or endnotes are added Word automatically numbers them. Word will automatically renumber footnote/endnote and reference marks whenever footnotes and endnotes are added, deleted or moved. Footnotes are only visible in Page Layout view.

Using Bookmarks, Captions and Cross-References

What you will learn in this unit

Bookmarks are the equivalent of strips of paper that you would put in a book so that you can find a particular page very quickly. If you wished to mark several places in a book you would make a brief note on the paper marker to remind you of the topic to be found on that page. You name electronic bookmarks in a similar manner so that you can easily find a particular point in a document.

A caption is the text that appears next to a table or figure: for example, 'Figure 1 Sales for South-West region'. By attaching a caption for the tables and figures in a document, Word automatically numbers them and renumber them when you revise the document and add, remove or rearrange your tables and figures.

If you wish to refer to a particular figure, table or other feature in a document then use a cross-reference. You may cross-reference across documents if the documents all belong to the same master document. Master documents are introduced in the Unit 7.

At the end of this unit you will be able to:

❑ Add, find and delete bookmarks in a document.

❑ Use a bookmark to create an index entry that contains a page range.

❑ Add and remove a caption.

❑ Use Auto Caption.

❑ Create a cross-reference.

Bookmarks

Bookmarks are used to mark a location in a document so that you can:

❑ 'Jump' to that location.

❑ Refer to it in a cross-reference; this will be considered in the section on cross-references.

❑ Use the location to generate a range of pages for an index entry.

Adding, jumping to and deleting bookmarks

Bookmarks do not appear on-screen by default but they can be made visible if required. Insert a bookmark as follows:

1. Either select the text you wish to bookmark or position the insertion point next to it and choose **Insert-Bookmark**.

2. Key in a name for the bookmark and click on the **Add** button. Repeat this process to add all the bookmarks required in the document. Note that bookmark names can be up to 40 characters in length but that spaces in them are not allowed.

   To move (jump) to a bookmark choose **Edit-Go To** and select **Bookmark** from the **Go to What** list; open the list of bookmark names, select the one you want and click on **Go To**.

   To delete a bookmark choose **Insert-Bookmark** and highlight the name of the bookmark you want to delete, then click on the **Delete** button.

To delete a bookmark and all the text associated with that bookmark, select all the text and then press *Delete*.

Making bookmarks visible

You can show bookmarks that have been added to a document:

1. First change to Normal view using **View-Normal**.

2. Choose **Tools-Options** and select the **View** tab. Tick the **Bookmarks** check box in the **Show** section and click on **OK**. Bookmarks will be shown enclosed by square brackets.

3. To make the bookmarks invisible again, remove the tick from the **Bookmarks** check box.

You may add a bookmark at the insertion point without selecting any text; if you display this bookmark, it will appear as a large **I** as the brackets are on top of each other.

Task 1: Adding and jumping to bookmarks

1. Create the document **Letting** (which is an abbreviated version of the full document for illustration purposes), as shown below.

2. Select the heading *Do I have to pay tax on the rent I receive* and choose **Insert-Bookmark**.

A Guide to Letting your Home

Deciding whether to let or sell

If you are currently undecided as to whether to let your property or sell it, then it's worth bearing in mind the increasing demand for good quality, rented accommodation.

Although home purchase is an attractive and very affordable option these days, an increasing number of people are choosing to rent – either as an alternative to buying, an intermediary step before embarking on the home ownership ladder, or simply because personal circumstances make renting the most practical solution.

So letting is an attractive option, as in our experience there is always a steady demand for good quality property let at sensible rents.

Professionals who care

If you have a residential property to let then it makes economic and practical sense to put the letting in the hands of experts such as Chelmer Estates Property Services.

Our highly specialised Residential Letting and Management Services help safeguard your interests and protect your property during the letting period.

How much will it cost?

Our letting and management fees are agreed at the start of any contract and are normally based on a percentage of rent. VAT is also payable.

Do I have to pay tax on the rent I receive?

This depends on your personal circumstances – mainly whether you are resident in the UK for tax purposes or a non-resident living abroad.

Need to know more?

Chelmer Estates Property Services has many years' experience in the lettings market, so if you have any further queries about the ins and outs of becoming a landlord – or even buying a property with a view to letting – come and discuss your needs with our staff who'll be happy to give you the very best advice, and provide you with our Landlord's Information Pack.

Decided to sell?

If you decide to sell your property at some point in the future, Chelmer Estates Property Services can offer you a comprehensive range of services, designed to sell your home for the best possible price, in the shortest possible time. Ask staff for our brochure, Guide to Selling your Home, for more details.

3. Enter the name *Tax_on_rent* for the bookmark and click on **Add**. Don't use spaces in the name; use the underscore symbol instead.

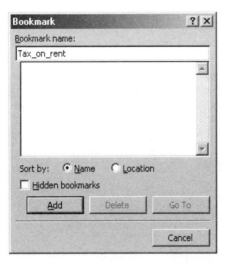

4. Repeat this for several other headings in the document, choosing suitable bookmark names each time. Save the document.

5. Choose **Edit-Go to**, select **Bookmark** from the **Go to What** list, open the list of bookmark names, select *Tax_on_rent* and click on **Go To**.

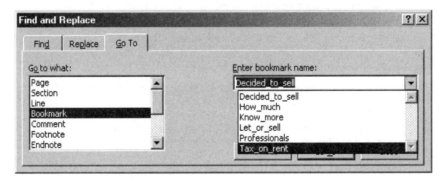

6. Make the bookmarks visible. First switch to Normal view using **View-Normal**. Then choose **Tools-Options**, tick the **Bookmarks** check box and click on **OK**. Review the document with the bookmarks visible, then make them invisible again by removing the tick from the **Bookmarks** check box.

[How much will it cost?]

Our letting and management fees are agreed at the start of any contract and are normally based on a percentage of rent. VAT is also payable.

[Do I have to pay tax on the rent I receive?]

This depends on your personal circumstances – mainly whether you are resident in the UK for tax purposes or a non-resident living abroad.

7. Try deleting one of your bookmarks by choosing **Insert-Bookmark**, highlighting the name of the bookmark to be removed and clicking on the **Delete** button.

8. Save and close the document.

Captions

Word can automatically add numbered captions when you insert pictures, tables, charts and other items. For example, as you insert tables Word can add the captions 'Table 1', 'Table 2' and so on.

Insert a caption as follows:

1. Select the item that you want to add a caption to and choose **Insert-Caption**.

2. Choose the label required from the drop-down **Label** list box. If the label you require is not in the list then click on the **New Label** button and key in the text of the label you require: for example, *Chart* (without the chart number). The new label will be added to the list ready for the next time you want to add a caption.

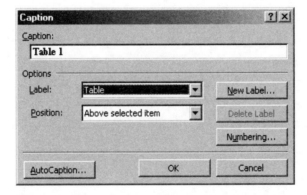

Note that you may remove any added labels from the list by choosing the label and clicking on the **Delete Label** button.

3. Select the position of the caption as either above or below the selected item.

4. If you wish, you may change the style of numbering using the **Numbering** button to display the Caption Numbering dialog box.

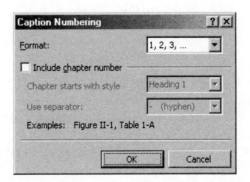

Different number formats include letters and Roman numerals as used in page numbering.

Task 2: Adding a caption

This task experiments with the use of captions.

1. Create the document below, which comprises three tables. The first table shows the number of new properties being offered for sale during the last quarter of the year, the second table the number of properties sold and the third table the average length of time properties remain on the books. Save the document as *Captions*.

Price range £000's	October	November	December
0-50	6	8	3
50-100	4	7	2
100-150	2	0	1
150-200	0	1	1
200 and above	0	0	0

Price range £000's	October	November	December
0-50	8	6	5
50-100	6	7	3
100-150	0	3	2
150-200	1	0	1
200 and above	1	0	0

Price range £000's	Weeks
0-50	10
50-100	13
100-150	12
150-200	20
200 and above	25

2. Click anywhere in the first table and choose **Insert-Caption**.

3. If necessary, choose **Table** as the option in the **Label** drop-down list box.

4. Accept the position of the caption as above the selected item. If you wish, you may add some additional text in the **Caption** box after *Table 1* by clicking at the end of the existing caption: for example, *New additions*. Click on **OK**.

5. Click in the second table and using **Insert-Caption** add a caption to this table. Notice that Word increments the table number. You could add the text ***Properties sold*** to this caption. Add a caption to the third table (***Average time on books***) and save.

6. Select the last table and its caption and cut and paste it (or drag and drop) between Tables 1 and 2. Select the whole document (**Edit-Select All**) and press *F9* to update the caption numbering. Now return the new Table 2 to the end of the document and renumber the tables.

Auto Caption

You may automatically add a caption to a table, figure, equation or other item when inserting it.

1. Choose **Insert-Caption** and click on **Auto Caption**.

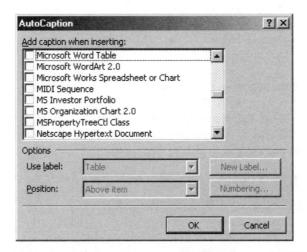

2. Select the items you want to be captioned automatically when you insert them in a document.

3. Select the options you want. Captions will now be inserted when you add any of the types of item selected in the AutoCaption dialog box.

Updating caption numbering following document revision

A table (or other captioned object) can be added to a document which already contains captioned tables (or other captioned objects of the same type as the one being added). If the new table is added between existing tables, it is given a caption and the following tables will have their caption numbers updated. However, if you delete a caption (by selecting and deleting) or if you rearrange the captioned objects in the document, then you will discover that the caption numbers are out of sequence. The caption numbers are fields and they are easily updated; simply select the whole document and press *F9*.

Cross-references

If you create a document that contains tables, charts, figures, numbered paragraphs etc. they are generally discussed in the text of the body of the document: for example, 'as illustrated in Figure 3'. Instead of typing the words 'Figure 3' you may insert a cross-reference to the figure. This is useful if you later modify the figure number as the document is revised, because when you update all the fields in the document the cross-reference will update and therefore still refer to the correct figure.

Clicking on a cross-reference will 'jump' to the referenced item, provided the **Insert as Hyperlink** check box was ticked when the cross-reference was created, which may be useful for proof-reading purposes.

Create a cross-reference as follows:

1. In the document, type the introductory text that begins the cross-reference. For example: 'as illustrated in'.

2. Choose **Insert-Cross-reference** and the Cross-reference dialog box appears.

3. The drop-down **Reference type** list box allows you to select the type of item you want to refer to – for example, a figure or table. If you have created custom captioned items (e.g. charts) then these will be listed as well.

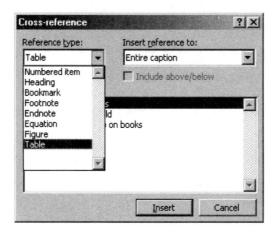

4. The drop-down **Insert reference to** list box allows you to choose the format of the cross-reference you want inserted in the document – for example, a chapter heading or just the caption name and number.

5. In the **For which caption** box, select the specific item you want to refer to. For example, if you chose **Chart** in the **Reference type** box and the document has three charts, select the chart you want to refer to.

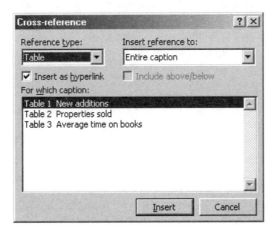

6. Click on the **Insert** button.

If you see an entry that looks something like *(REF Ref249586 * MERGEFORMAT)* instead of text, Word is displaying field codes instead of field results. To see the field results, click the field code with the right mouse button, and then click **Toggle Field Codes** on the shortcut menu.

If the item you want to refer to is located in another document, then both documents must be part of a master document. Master documents are discussed in Units 8 and 9.

Task 3: Adding a cross-reference

1. Open the document *Captions* created in the Task 2.

2. At the end of the table add the text *In*.

3. Choose **Insert-Cross-reference** and select **Table** from the drop-down **Reference type** list box.

4. Choose *Table 1* from the **For which caption** box and choose **Only label and number** from the **Insert reference to** box.

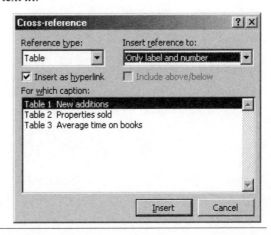

5. With **Insert as Hyperlink** checked, click on **Insert** and **Close**. Continue the text of the sentence *the number of new properties appearing on our books is shown*.

6. Add two similar sentences with cross-references to Tables 2 and 3 respectively.

7. What would you expect to happen if you were to move the tables around as at the end of the last task? Try it to see the power of cross-referencing.

Outlining a Document

What you will learn in this unit

Outlining, contents pages and indexes are useful approaches to structuring long documents. If you are creating long corporate documents you should think about their structure at an early stage in their creation.

Outlining is a technique for viewing a document at various levels of its structure. By viewing major headings, without accompanying text (this is hidden), it is possible to check the structure and flow of topics in a document. An Outline view looks like a table of contents. Further, Word can create a table of contents using the document headings.

For long documents, indexes may be useful in allowing your reader to 'look up' specific items in the document. An index refers them to the page (or pages) in the document where they will find the item discussed, exactly like the index you find at the end of a book.

At the end of this unit you will be able to:

❑   Apply heading styles so that you can use outlining.

❑   Add a table of contents to a document.

❑   Add an index to a document.

What you need

To complete this unit you will need:

❑   The document file *Letting* created in Unit 5

Outlining

If your document is more than a few paragraphs long then you should use headings. Word provides nine heading styles and these should be applied as styles to the headings in the document. *Heading 1* is the most important and *Heading 9* the least important. These levels of importance can also be given to any style, not just a heading style, by using the **Outline level** drop-down list box in the Paragraph dialog box.

Applying heading styles to headings is the basis for both using outlining as well as creating a table of contents. Outlining is a technique whereby a document is

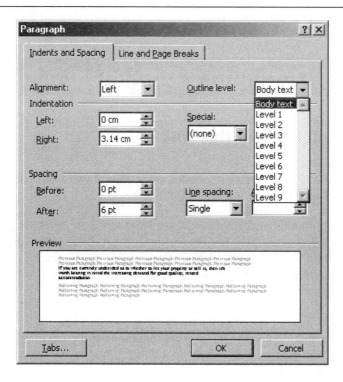

planned by noting the headings for the topics that are to be covered in the document. Topics can then be grouped under major headings and their order in the document arranged. Before word processors this kind of planning took place on paper, and any restructuring could be a time consuming manual process, particularly if most of the document had been handwritten or hand-typed.

Word processors have automated this outlining technique and so a document structure can be reworked at any stage of its production process. In Word, using Outline view, a document may be viewed in its entirety or at particular heading levels, with subordinate text being hidden. For example, if only heading level 1 is chosen, only the headings with the style *Heading 1* will be displayed. It is easy to display whatever level of outlining is required and it is also easy to move sections of text from one part of the document to another.

Task 1: Applying heading styles

1. Open the document *Letting*.

2. Apply the style *Heading 1* to the main heading and *Heading 2* to the sub-heading.

3. Change the *Heading 1* style to 14 point bold centred and *Heading 2* to 11 point left-aligned.

Outline view

To see the document in outline choose **View-Outline** and the document will take on a different appearance. The Outlining toolbar appears.

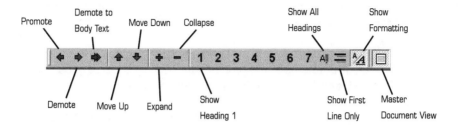

The buttons on this toolbar allow you to:

❏ Promote or demote a heading level.

❏ Demote a heading to normal 'body text', i.e. no heading level.

❏ Move a heading (and its subordinate text) up or down within the document.

❏ Expand or collapse a selected level so that you can choose whether or not to see subordinate levels and text.

❏ Show the levels of headings; for example, **3** will show all *Heading 1*, *Heading 2* and *Heading 3* levels of text; **All** will show all the text (with associated outlining symbols).

❏ Show the first line only; this allows you to see the opening line of subordinate text if that text is longer than one line.

❏ Show formatting; you can choose to see the formatting as used in the document or to ignore it; heading levels are indented in Outline view so you may prefer not to see the formatting; heading styles can be changed just as in other views.

❏ Switch to Master Document view. Master documents are the subject of Units 7 and 8.

Outlining symbols

When a document is displayed in Outline view, the heading and text are shown indented: the larger the indent, the higher (but less important) the heading level. Each heading or text is prefixed by an outlining symbol as seen in the table below.

Symbol	Meaning
✿	The heading has associated subordinate text
▭	The heading does not have subordinate text
▫	Prefixes the first line of a paragraph of body text

Task 2: Viewing and manipulating a document in Outline view

1. Open the document *Letting* and choose **View-Outline**.

2. Click on the **Show Heading 1** button to see just the one heading at this level. Try clicking on the other heading level buttons to display the document outline. Click on **Show First Line Only**.

3. Display both heading levels. Position the insertion point on a level 2 heading and click on the **Promote** button to promote this heading to level 1. Use the **Demote** button to put it back to level 4. Finally, restore it to level 2.

4. With both levels of heading displayed in Outline view, position the insertion point in the heading *Professionals who care* and click on the **Expand** button to display the text at this level. Click on the **Collapse** button to collapse the text. Expanding and collapsing of text can also be accomplished by double-clicking on the symbol prefixing the heading. Experiment with expanding and collapsing text and levels in this document.

   If you expand or collapse a level that has subordinate levels, then expanding and collapsing works one level at a time and affects all subordinate levels.

5. Return the display to the two levels of heading. Position the insertion point in the *How much will it cost?* heading and click on the **Move Up** button. This moves the heading and its collapsed subordinate text (and levels) with it. Use **Edit-Undo** to return the document to its original order.

   Clicking and dragging the outline prefix symbol is another way in which the text can be re-ordered.

6. Toggle the **Show Formatting** button to switch between displaying heading formatting or not.

7. Click on **Show All Headings** to display the whole document in Outline view. Toggle the **Show First Line Only** button and note its effect. Investigate collapsing and expanding levels with first line only switched on and off.

8. Return the document to its original formatting. The easiest way is to close it without saving.

   Note that we have used outlining with an existing document in this task. You could create a new document using Outline view and key in headings and arrange their order and levels before adding text. It is easy to switch from one view to another (Normal to Outline) and back, to work either on text creation or document structure.

Creating a simple table of contents

Outline view resembles a table of contents, especially when only the major heading levels are displayed; only the page numbers are missing. Word uses the headings and notes their page numbers and thereby creates a table of contents.

To create a table of contents, open a document, choose **Insert-Index and Tables** and click on the **Table of Contents** tab. You may select from a variety of formats and you can decide how many heading levels you want in your table of contents. After inserting the table of contents, you can change its format.

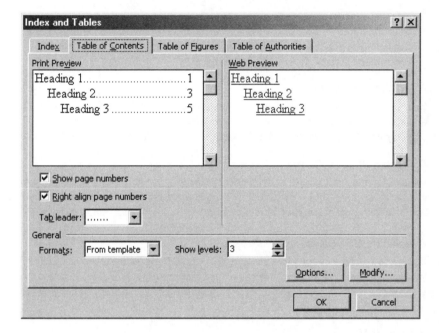

Task 3: Creating a table of contents

A simple table of contents is to be created for the document *Code of Practice*, shown below. For brevity, only a few lines from each section have been included.

1. Type in the text and save the document as *Code of Practice*. Format the main heading as *Heading 1*, the sub-headings as *Heading 2*. Modify the *Heading 2* style so the **Page break before** is ticked on the **Line and Page Breaks** tab of the Paragraph dialog.

2. Position the insertion point at the beginning of the document. Choose **Insert-Index and Tables**. Click on the **Table of Contents** tab.

3. Set the **Show levels** value to **2**. Select the **From Template** format for the table of contents and click on **OK**. The table of contents will be inserted at the beginning of the document.

Code of Practice

1. General

This Code applies to estate agency services in the United Kingdom for the selling and buying of residential property.

2. Instructions

By law you must give your client written confirmation of his instructions to act in the buying or selling of properties on his behalf.

3. For Sale Boards

You can only erect a 'For Sale' board with the client's permission. When you put up a 'For Sale' board you must keep to the Town and Country Planning (Control of Advertisements) Regulations 1992 as amended.

4. Published Material

You must take all reasonable steps to make sure that all statements, whether oral or written, made about a property are accurate. Whenever possible, the written details of a property must be sent to the Seller for them to confirm that the details are accurate.

5. Offers

By law you must tell clients as soon as is reasonably possible about all offers that you receive at any time until contracts have been exchanged unless the offer is an amount or type which the client has specifically instructed you, in writing, not to pass on.

6. Access to Premises

Unless you and the client agree otherwise in writing, if you hold the keys to a property you must accompany anyone looking around that property. If you are arranging for someone to view an occupied property, you must agree the arrangements with the occupier beforehand, wherever possible.

7. Clients' Money

You must not hold a deposit or any other money belonging to a client, unless you are covered by adequate insurance.

8. Conflict of Interest

If your firm is instructed to sell a property and you, an employee or an associate is intending to buy it, you must, before negotiations begin, give all the relevant facts, in writing, to the client and his solicitor.

9. Financial Services

You must keep to the rules of the recognised self-regulating organisation (as defined under the Financial Services Act 1986) which regulates the conduct of your investment business, or the life assurance company you represent, as the case may be.

10. Interpretation and Definitions

In this Code, references to the masculine include the feminine, the plural and organisations.

Tables of contents may be put anywhere, so take care where you position the insertion point; usually they are placed at the beginning of a document and sometimes in a separate section, so as not to interfere with page numbering.

4. Insert a hard page break between the table of contents and the main heading. Save the document.

--Page Break--

Code of Practice

1. General

This Code applies to estate agency services in the United Kingdom for the selling and buying of residential property.

2. Instructions

Updating and removing a table of contents

Should the document be revised, the table of contents can be updated by positioning the insertion point in the table of contents and pressing *F9*. You will be given the choice of updating either just the page numbers or the whole table of contents.

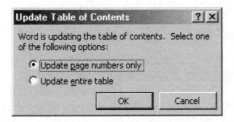

A table of contents can be removed by simply highlighting the table and pressing the *Delete* key. If you click in the left margin, level with the first line of your table of contents, the whole table should highlight.

You can use a table of contents to jump to a specific heading in your document, by double-clicking on the page number of the heading to which you wish to go.

Creating an index

An index is an alphabetical list of important words or phrases that occur in your document, along with the page numbers where you will find the word or phrase used in the document. An index is usually found at the end of the document.

To create an index, you must first go through your document and mark important words or phrases as index entries. When all the index entries have been marked, you can build the finished index, selecting an index design of your choice. Word then collects the index entries, sorts them alphabetically, references their page numbers, finds and removes duplicate entries from the same page, and creates the index in the document.

Marking an index entry

To mark an index entry:

1. Highlight the word or phrase you wish to mark as an entry. Choose **Insert-Index and Tables**, select the **Index** tab and click on the **Mark Entry** button. The Mark Index Entry dialog box appears; to mark the entry click on **Mark**.

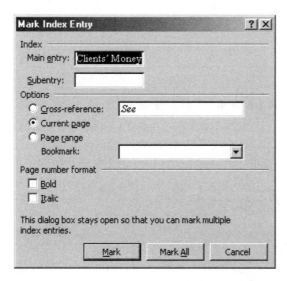

2. The Mark Index Entry box remains open so that you may scroll through the document and add all the index marks. Each time you add a mark highlight the relevant word, click in the **Main entry** box and click on **Mark**. If the high-

lighted word appears several times throughout the document and you want to mark all the occurrences then click on the **Mark All** button. The entries are inserted in the document as hidden fields.

▪ *7.·Clients'·Money{·XE·"Clients'·Money"·}¶*

You·must·not·hold·a·deposit·or·any·other·money·belonging·to·a·client,·unless·you·are· covered·by·adequate·insurance.¶

▪ *8.·Conflict·of·Interest{·XE·"Conflict·of·Interest"·}¶*

If·your·firm·is·instructed·to·sell·a·property·and·you,·an·employee·or·an·associate·is· intending·to·buy·it,·you·must,·before·negotiations·begin,·give·all·the·relevant·facts,·in· writing,·to·the·client·and·his·solicitor.¶

▪ *9.·Financial·Services{·XE·"Financial·Services"·}¶*

You·must·keep·to·the·rules·of·the·recognised·self-regulating·organisation·(as·defined· under·the·Financial·Services·Act·1986)·which·regulates·the·conduct·of·your·investment· business,·or·the·life·assurance·company·you·represent,·as·the·case·may·be.¶

▪ *10.·Interpretation{·XE·"Interpretation"·}·and·Definitions{·XE·"Definitions"·}¶*

In·this·Code,·references·to·the·masculine·include·the·feminine,·the·plural·and· organisations.¶

---

3. When you have finished click on **Close**. Click on the ¶ button to hide the fields and formatting characters.

Adding the index

When you have marked all the index entries, move to the end of the document and choose **Insert-Index and Tables**, select the **Index** tab, select a format for the index

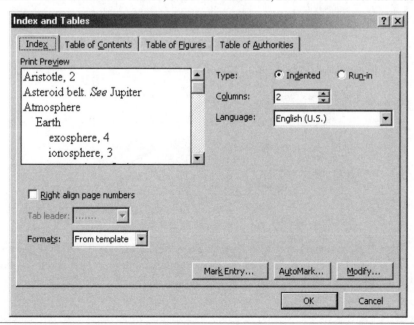

and click on **OK**. The index will be inserted in a separate section. You can change the format after the index has been inserted.

Updating and removing an index

Should the document be revised the index can be updated by positioning the insertion point in the index and pressing *F9*.

You can edit any index entry by clicking on the ¶ button to display the fields and then changing the text in quotes in the *XE* field. To remove an index entry, delete the *XE* field.

In Normal view, if you click on the top section break marker, the whole index and its section break should highlight. Press *Delete* to remove the index and section break.

Task 4: Creating an index

1. Open the document *Letting* (as amended in Task 2). Modify the *Heading 2* style so that there is a page break before each sub-heading.

2. Highlight the phrase 'let or sell' in the first sub-heading and choose **Insert-Index and Tables**. Select the **Index** tab and click on the **Mark Entry** button. Change the first letter in the **Main entry** box to a capital. Click on **Mark** to mark this entry.

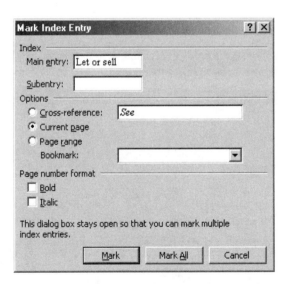

3. With the Mark Index Entry box open, select the word 'rent' in the second paragraph. Click in the **Main entry** box, capitalise the first letter and then click on **Mark All**.

4. Choose several other words which you think would be suitable in the index and either use **Mark** or **Mark All** to add them to your index entries. When you have finished click on **Close**. Click on ¶ .

5. Move to the end of the document. On a blank line, choose **Insert-Index and Tables**, select the **Index** tab, select the **From template** format and click on **OK**. The index will be inserted in a separate section. Save and close the document.

---

time. Ask staff for our brochure, Guide to Selling your Home, for more details.

··Section Break (Continuous)··············

Chelmer Estates Property Services, 3
Guide to Selling your Home, 7
Landlord's Information Pack, 6
Let or sell, 2
Letting, 2
Management fees, 4
Rent, 2, 4, 5
Selling your property, 7
Tax, 5
VAT, 4

··Section Break (Continuous)··············

Using a bookmark to create an index entry that contains a page range

When you want an index entry to indicate a range of pages instead of a single page, you must mark that page range with a bookmark.

1. In the document, select the range of text you want the index entry to refer to, and then choose **Insert-Bookmark**.

2. In the **Bookmark Name** box, enter a name and click on **Add**.

3. In the document, click the text that you marked with a bookmark.

4. Press *Alt+Shift+X*.

5. In the **Main Entry** box, enter the index entry for the marked text.

6. Select **Page Range**. In the **Bookmark** box, type or select the bookmark name for the range of pages from step 2.

7. Click on **Mark**. When you use **Insert-Index and Tables** to add an index this page range will be included.

The index entry can be removed in the same way as ordinary index entries: that is, by selecting the entry and pressing *Delete*.

Task 5: Using a bookmark to create an index entry that contains a page range

1. Open the document *Letting* and select the range of text containing the sections *How much will it cost?* and *Do I have to pay tax on the rent I receive?* Choose **Insert-Bookmark**.

2. In the **Bookmark Name** box, enter **Costs** and then click on **Add**. Position the insertion point at the end of the first heading of the bookmarked range. Press *Alt-Shift-X*.

3. Enter the name **Costs** for the **Main entry**. Select the **Page Range** option, open the drop-down bookmark list box and choose *Tenancy*. Click on **Mark** and **Close**.

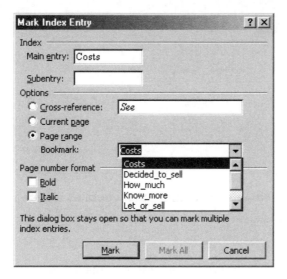

4. Move to the end of the document and update the index by clicking in it and pressing *F9*.

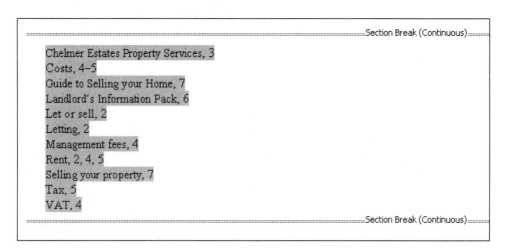

Unit 7

Creating a Master Document

What you will learn in this unit

Word offers many automatic features for document completion, such as tables of contents and indexes. When you are producing a long document, it becomes more cumbersome to work with as it gets longer and it makes sense to break it into two or more shorter documents.

In order to be able to create a table of contents or index for more than one document, which together comprise a publication, the documents can be grouped together using a *master document*. The master document allows you to work with the group of documents as a whole or individually.

Documents grouped using a master document are known as *subdocuments*. By using a master document, you can easily create cross-references, a table of contents, and an index across all the subdocuments. You can also print several subdocuments without opening them individually.

At the end of this unit you will be able to:

❏ Create a new master document and subdocuments.

❏ Convert an existing document into a master document.

❏ Add existing documents as subdocuments to a master document.

❏ Add page numbering and headers and footers.

Different ways to view a Word document

Master Document view is used for working with the master document as a whole; the other Word views are used when working with individual files. A brief resumé of the different 'views' provided by Word is included here. The buttons to the left of the horizontal scrollbar are used to switch between the different views.

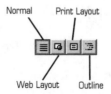

Normal view

In Word, Normal view is the usual view for a single document. It is the best all-purpose view for typing, editing and formatting text. Normal view shows text formatting but simplifies the layout of the page so that you can type and edit quickly.

Web Layout view

This view is designed for reading a document on-line. Text is displayed slightly larger and wraps to fit the window. If the document has heading styles, an outline of these can be displayed in a left-hand window by clicking on the **Document Map** button. This provides a useful way of moving around the document.

Print Layout view

In Print Layout view, you can see how objects will be positioned on the printed page. This view is useful for editing headers and footers, for adjusting margins and for working with columns, drawing objects and frames.

Outline view

Outline view makes it easy to look at the structure of a document and to move, copy and reorganise text. In Outline view, you can collapse a document to see only the main headings or you can expand it to see the entire document. Outline view also provides access to Master Document view.

Master Document view

The main function of Master Document view is to group several Word documents so that you can work with them as if they were one document. You can then make changes to the long document – such as adding an index or table of contents, or creating cross-references – without opening each of the individual documents.

By switching to Normal view from Master Document view, you can make specific changes to the subdocuments. In Normal view, each subdocument is displayed as a section of the master document.

Working with a master document

In Master Document view, the Master Document toolbar is displayed. This enables you to organise the subdocuments comprising your long document.

 The first two-thirds of the toolbar contain the outlining tools, described in Unit 6.

There are also additional buttons for subdocument control.

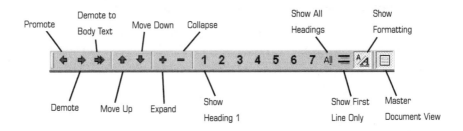

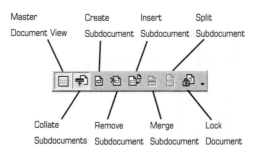

Creating a new master document with subdocuments

To create a new master document:

1. Open a new document in Word and choose **View-Outline**.

2. Type the outline for the master document. Use the built-in heading styles to create a heading for each subdocument. For example, you could use *Heading 1* for the document title and *Heading 2* for chapter titles. Alternatively create your own styles with the appropriate heading levels.

3. Select the headings and text you want to divide into subdocuments. Make sure that the first heading in the selection is the heading level you want to use at the beginning of each subdocument. For example, if your selection begins with *Heading 2*, Word creates a new subdocument at each *Heading 2* in the selected text.

4. On the Master Document toolbar, click on the **Create Subdocument** button. Word displays a box around each subdocument.

5. To save the new master document and all its subdocuments, choose **File-Save As**. Enter a filename and location for the master document. You will usually create a new directory for each sub-document. Word assigns a filename to each subdocument based on the first characters in the subdocument heading.

Task 1: Creating a new master document with subdocuments

This task and the following tasks relating to master documents will illustrate how a larger publication, such as a book, is produced. It is intended to take extracts from this book in these tasks to illustrate the features but without creating large amounts of text.

1. Open a new document in Word and choose **View-Master Document**. Key in the text as illustrated, using *Heading 1* for the main title and *Heading 2* for the chapter titles.

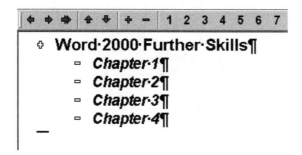

2. Select the four chapter headings and click on the **Create Subdocument** button to divide the document into four subdocuments. Each heading is surrounded by a box which has a subdocument icon in the top left corner.

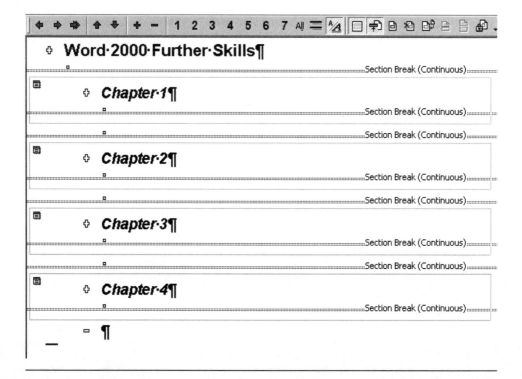

3. Choose **File-Save As**. Create and select a new directory called *Word 2000 Further Skills* for the master document. The filename should also be called *Word 2000 Further Skills*. Click on **Save**. Word assigns a filename to each subdocument based on the first characters in the subdocument heading.

4. Using Explorer you can verify that five files have been created: *Word 2000 Further Skills*, *Chapter 1*, *Chapter 2*, *Chapter 3* and *Chapter 4*.

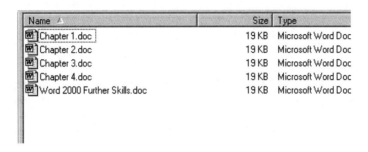

Working with subdocuments

You can open, edit and print any subdocument from within its master document. To open a subdocument in Master Document view, double-click its subdocument icon. If you delete or rename a subdocument, make sure you do so within its master document.

Task 2: Working with subdocuments

1. Open the master document *Word 2000 Further Skills*. The subdocuments are collapsed, so you will see a link to each document.

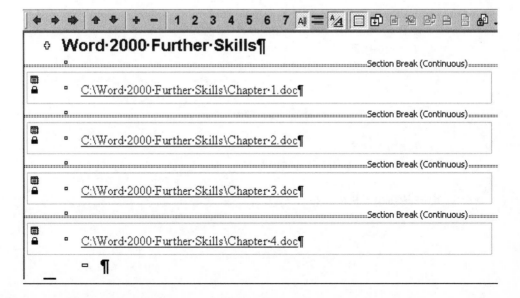

2. Click on the **Expand Subdocument** button. When the subdocuments are expanded the **Expand Subdocument** button toggles to the **Collapse Subdocuments** button.

3. Under the heading *Chapter 1* add the heading ***Checking spelling and grammar as you work*** and the relevant paragraph of text from Unit 1. Use a *Heading 3* style for the heading and *Normal* style for the paragraph text.

4. Under the *Chapter 2* heading add (from Unit 2) the heading ***Printing options*** (*Heading 3*), the heading ***Selecting a printer*** (*Heading 4*) and the first paragraph of text in each case. (The first time you use *Heading 4*, you will have to type it into the **Style** box.)

5. Under the *Chapter 3* heading add (from Unit 3) the heading ***Creating templates*** (*Heading 3*) and the first two sentences of the following paragraph. Save.

6. Investigate the outlining features available in Master Document view (refer to Unit 6 to remind yourself of these).

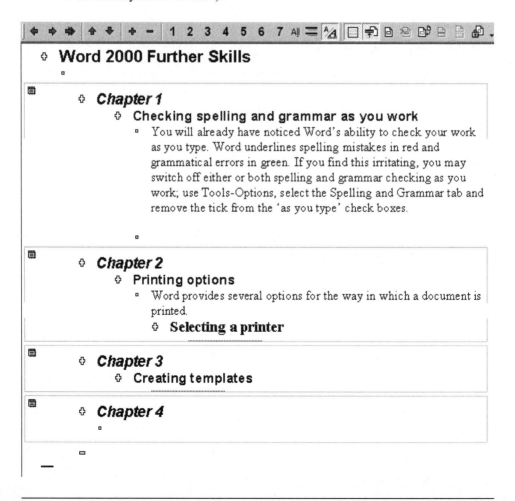

7. Double-click on the Subdocument icon in the top left-hand corner of the *Chapter 1* box to display this document separately. You can then work with the document in Normal or Page Layout view as you wish. Try adding some additional text, save and close. You will return to the master document.

8. With only the master document open try redefining the style *Heading 2*. This will alter the style in all the subdocuments. If you use a master document, you can use styles to ensure consistency across all the documents.

Converting an existing document to a master document or subdocument

Any Word document can be a master document or a subdocument. An existing document can be converted to a master document and other existing documents can be added as subdocuments. To convert an existing document to a master document:

1. Open the document you wish to convert and choose **View-Outline**.

2. Use the outlining buttons to promote, demote and arrange headings.

3. To prepare the document for division into subdocuments, use the built-in heading styles to create headings for each subdocument. For example, you could use *Heading 1* for each subdocument title.

4. Select the headings and text you want to divide into subdocuments. Make sure that the first heading in the selection is the heading level you want to use at the beginning of each subdocument.

5. On the Master Document toolbar, click on the **Create Subdocument** button.

6. Choose **File-Save As** to save the new master document and all its subdocuments. Enter a filename and location for the master document. Word assigns a filename to each subdocument based on the first characters in the subdocument heading. Keep the master document and subdocuments together in a folder of their own.

To insert an existing Word document into a master document as a subdocument:

1. Open the master document to which you want to add an existing Word document.

2. In Master Document view, with the subdocuments in expanded view, position the insertion point at the place where you want to add the existing document.

3. On the Master Document toolbar, click on the **Insert Subdocument** button.

4. Select the file you want to add and click on **Open**.

If the subdocument and the master document are based on different templates, or if they have different settings, the master document settings override the subdocument settings. If only the subdocument is opened, its settings are unchanged.

Task 3: Converting an existing document to a subdocument

1. Create a new document and add the title **Chapter 6** (*Heading 2*). From Unit 6, add the heading **Outlining** (*Heading 3*), with its associated first paragraph. Save this document as *Chapter 6* and close.

2. Open the master document *Word 2000 Further Skills*. Click on the **Expand Subdocuments** button. With the insertion point at the beginning, click on the **Insert Subdocument** button. Select the file *Chapter 6* and click on **Open**. This file has now become a subdocument. Save the master document. This document has been put in the wrong place deliberately; Unit 8 deals with rearranging subdocuments.

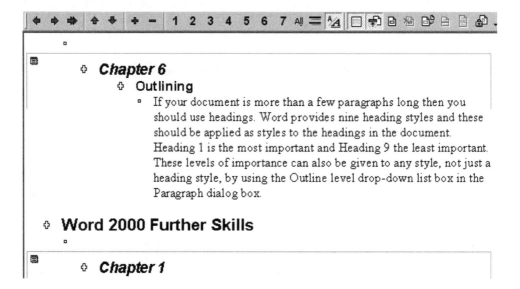

Note that styles in the master document are applied to the new document in Master Document view, even though they may be different in the underlying document itself.

Page numbering, headers and footers in master documents

A master document treats all the component subdocuments as separate sections so that you can control page numbering and headers and footers separately in each section, or you can have sequential page numbering throughout the whole master document. Sequential page numbering is investigated in the following task.

Task 4: Page numbering and headers and footers

1. Open the master document *Word 2000 Further Skills* and click on the **Expand Subdocuments** button. To make this task more realistic format the *Heading 2* style to be **Page break before**.

2. Use **View-Header and Footer** to insert a page number at the bottom of the page.

3. Use **View-Print Layout** to see the document as it would be printed and you should see that page numbers have been added. Note that **Same as Previous** has been set so that numbering is continuous throughout the sections comprising the whole document. If you wish to format the page numbering, use **View-Header and Footer**.

4. Try adding a header that is different for each chapter, e.g. *Chap 1* etc. You will need to click on the ▣ (**Same as Previous**) button each time to make the headers independent. Save and close.

Working with Master Documents

What you will learn in this unit

Master documents allow you to use a number of word processor features across a collection of documents. Before using these it is useful to be able to organise sub-documents and to protect them from accidental (or deliberate) revision.

At the end of this unit you will be able to:

❏ Use outlining to display and print a master document.

❏ Reorganise and rearrange subdocuments.

❏ Protect subdocuments.

❏ Create tables of contents, indexes, bookmarks and cross-references.

What you need

To complete this unit you will need:

❏ The master document file *Word 2000 Further Skills* created in Unit 7

Using outlining to view a master document's organisation

If you formatted headings with the built-in heading styles, you can review the organisation of a document in Outline View by collapsing the subordinate text below the headings.

To collapse	Do this
Text below a specific heading level	On the Outlining toolbar, click the numbered button for the lowest level of heading you want to display. For example, click the button labelled **3** to display heading levels 1 – 3.
All subheadings and body text under a heading	Double-click the ✛ next to the heading.
Text under a heading, one level at a time	Click the heading text and then click the **Collapse** button on the Outlining toolbar.

To collapse	Do this
All body text	On the Outlining toolbar, click on the **All** button.
All headings and body text	On the Outlining toolbar, click on the **All** button.
All collapsed subheadings and body text under a heading	Double-click the ✛ next to the heading.
Only the first line of body text	On the Outlining toolbar, click on **Show First Line Only**. An ellipsis (...) after the first line indicates that additional lines of text are collapsed.
Collapsed text under a heading, one level at a time	Click the heading text and then click the **Expand** button on the Outlining toolbar.

If you select a heading that has collapsed subordinate text or select a heading by clicking its ✛ symbol, the subordinate text is also selected. Any editing, such as moving, copying, or deleting, also affects the subordinate text.

Printing a master document

You can print just part of a master document:

1. To specify the amount of detail you want printed, display the master document in Master Document view.

2. Using the guidelines in the tables above, expand or collapse headings to display as much of the document as you want to print.

3. Choose **File-Print** and set your required printing options.

To print the entire document, display the master document in Normal view, add page numbering or any other headers and footers and use **File-Print** as usual to print the entire document.

Task 1: Printing a master document

1. Open the master document *Word 2000 Further Skills*. Expand the subdocuments. Display only the first two heading levels.

2. Choose **File-Print** and click on **OK** to print this Outline view. You may wish to try expanding one or two of the levels and then print the document again.

3. Now view the document in Normal view or Page Layout view. Using **File-Print** will enable you to print the entire document as if it were one document.

Rearranging subdocuments within a master document

To rearrange subdocuments:

1. Display the master document in Master Document view.

2. Select the headings you want to move. To select an entire subdocument, click on its subdocument icon.

3. Drag the selected headings to the new location. As you drag you will see a horizontal line with an arrow indicating the potential drop position. Remember that all subordinate text and headings will move with the selected heading. Headings and associated text may be dragged from one subdocument to another.

Renaming a subdocument

To rename a subdocument, display the master document in Master Document view. Open the subdocument you want to rename, by double-clicking on its Subdocument icon. Choose **File-Save As** and enter a new filename for the subdocument. Close the subdocument, redisplaying the master document. Collapse the subdocuments to see the new name in the hyperlink.

 Important Do not use any other means to rename a document that is a subdocument of a master document. If you use Windows Explorer or MS-DOS to rename or move such a document, the master document will no longer be able to find or recognise the subdocument.

Removing a subdocument from a master document

To remove a subdocument, display the master document in Master Document view. Select the subdocument you want to remove, by clicking on its subdocument icon, and press *Delete*. Note that when you remove a subdocument from a master document, the subdocument file still exists in its original location.

Merging subdocuments

To merge two or more subdocuments:

1. Display the master document in Master Document view. If necessary, rearrange the subdocuments so that they are next to one another in the master document.

2. Click on the subdocument icon of the first subdocument you want to merge.

3. To select the next subdocument, hold down the **Shift** key and click on the subdocument icon. If you wish to merge more than two subdocuments, repeat this process for each subdocument you want to merge.

4. On the Master Document toolbar, click on the **Merge Subdocuments** button. Note that when you save the master document, Word saves the merged subdocuments with the filename of the first subdocument.

Splitting a subdocument into two subdocuments

To splilt a subdocument, display the master document in Master Document view. Using the built-in heading styles, create a heading for the new subdocument. Select the new heading. On the Master Document toolbar click on the **Split Subdocument** button.

Converting a subdocument into part of the master document

Display the master document in Master Document view and view the subdocuments in expanded view. If the subdocument to be converted is locked, unlock it by clicking on the **Lock Document** button. Locking and unlocking is discussed in more detail later in this unit.

Click on the subdocument icon of the subdocument you want to make part of the master document. Click on the **Remove Subdocument** button on the Master Document toolbar. When you convert a subdocument into part of a master document, the subdocument file still exists in its original location.

Task 2: Rearranging subdocuments

To rearrange subdocuments:

1. Open the master document *Word 2000 Further Skills*. Copy the blank line from the top of the master document to the bottom.

2. Keep the subdocuments collapsed and select the entire subdocument *Chapter 6* by clicking on its subdocument icon.

3. Drag the selected subdocument icon to the end of the master document. Investigate the effect on the headers and footers. Save and close.

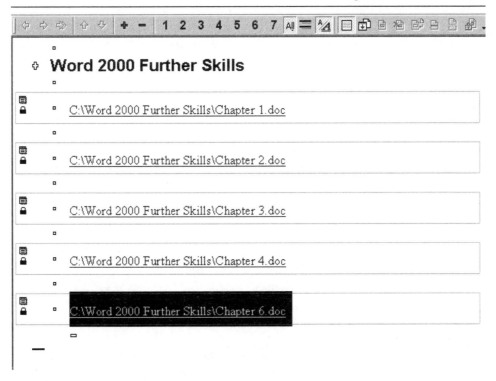

Locking or unlocking a master document or subdocument

Locking a document will prevent unintentional changes being made to the document. You can lock the entire master document or you can lock subdocuments individually. Locking the master document does not lock the subdocuments. To edit a locked document you need to unlock it first.

To lock or unlock a master document, display the master document in Master Document View and click anywhere in the master document (but not any of the subdocuments); to lock or unlock a subdocument, click anywhere in the expanded subdocument. Then click on the **Lock Document** button on the Master Document toolbar.

When a master document is locked, it is marked as *(Read-Only)* in the title bar. When a subdocument is locked, the subdocument icon displays a padlock icon below it.

Limiting access for changing a master document or a subdocument

Just as for any other Word document you can password-protect your documents if you are working in a shared environment. Use **File-Save As** and click on the **Options** button, then set and retype a password for the document.

Task 3: Locking and unlocking

1. Using the master document *Word 2000 Further Skills*, expand the subdocuments and add some text to the master document: for example, additional text on the title page at the beginning.

2. Investigate the effect of locking and unlocking the master document and subdocuments.

Creating a table of contents for a master document

To create a table of contents:

1. Display the master document in Master Document view.

2. Expand the subdocuments.

3. Position the insertion point at the place where you want to insert the table of contents, which should normally be at the end of the title page but before the first subdocument icon. Insert a hard page break.

4. Create the table of contents as for a normal document by choosing **Insert-Index and Tables** and then selecting the **Table of Contents** tab. Set the **Show Levels** value to 2. Click on **OK**.

5. Collapse the subdocuments and save.

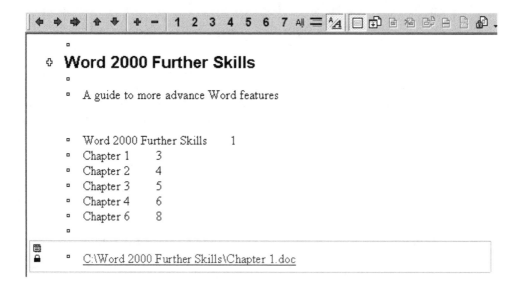

Creating index entries and index

To create an index:

1. Display the master document in Master Document view.

2. Expand the subdocuments.

3. Add index entries to the subdocuments as you would for ordinary documents. If necessary refer back to Unit 7.

4. Create the index by positioning the insertion point at the place where you want to insert the finished index. This would usually be at the end of the master document.

5. Choose **Insert-Tables and Index** and then select the **Index** tab to choose the index format you require.

6. Collapse the subdocuments and save.

C:\Word 2000 Further Skills\Chapter 6.doc

- Checking spelling, 3
- Creating templates, 5
- Grammar, 3
- Outlining, 8
- Printers, 4
- Printing options, 4
- Selecting a printer, 4
- Spelling, 3
- Templates, 5

Using bookmarks, captions and cross-references in master documents

To add bookmarks, captions and cross-references:

1. Open the master document and expand the subdocuments.

2. Switch to Normal view.

3. Create the bookmarks, captions and cross-references as described in Unit 5. Note that you can only create cross-references to other subdocuments within the same master document.

Task 4: Investigating tables of contents, indexes, bookmarks and cross-references in master documents

1. Open *Word 2000 Further Skills* in Master Document view and expand the subdocuments. Position the insertion point before the *Chapter 1* subdocument (after the title page). Check that the document is unlocked. Choose **Insert-Tables and Index**. Select the **Table of Contents** tab and heading level 2, select a style and click on **OK**. Change to Normal or Page Layout view to see the table of contents.

2. Switch back to Master Document view and move through the subdocuments (unlock them first) and select and mark various words to go in an index. Refer back to Unit 7 to see how to do this. Move to the end of the document and choose **Insert-Tables and Index**. Select the **Index** tab, choose the style of index and click on **OK**.

3. Click on the subdocument icon for *Chapter 4* to open the document. Add one of the tables from Unit 5 Task 3. Using **Insert-Caption** add a caption to this table (as in Unit 5). Save and close *Chapter 4*.

4. In Master Document view add the text **The data is shown in** to the subdocument *Chapter 3*. Using **Insert-Cross reference** select *Table 1* from the list.

⬦ ***Chapter 3***
    ⬦ **Creating templates**
        ▫ A template is a predefined format for a document. A template can be used to define not only standard text but also aspects such as the font, borders, page size and orientation.
        ▫ The data is shown in Table 1.

⬦ ***Chapter 4***
    ▫ Table 1

Price range £000's	October	November	December
0-50	6	8	3
50-100	4	7	2
100-150	2	0	1
150-200	0	1	1
200 and above	0	0	0

5. In Master Document view try adding bookmarks for all the chapter headings. (Refer to Unit 5.) Save all the documents.

6. Experiment further with these documents but do not save them.

Using Office Applications Together

What you will learn in this unit

All the Office applications are powerful and often you can use them to produce documents for which they were not originally designed, such as slides from Word or a sales report from Excel. However, the purpose of a suite of applications is to allow you to switch to the appropriate application for the task in hand and to embed or link data from other applications.

If you installed Microsoft Office, you can use the Office Binder to keep related files together. For example, if you have a Word document, a Microsoft Excel work-book and PowerPoint slides that make up a single report, you can place them in a binder to work on them together. This is a useful organisational tool.

This unit will demonstrate some of the ways in which Office applications can be used. By the end of this unit you will be able to:

❑   Use Word's facility to insert an Excel worksheet.

❑   Create a PowerPoint presentation from a Word outline.

❑   Use embedding and linking.

What you need

To complete this unit you will need:

❑   The document file *Letting* created in Unit 6 and amended in Unit 7

Inserting an Excel worksheet

If you wish to add a table of figures to your document and you want to be able to perform more than simple calculations upon them, you can insert an Excel work-sheet. This can be done without having to start Excel separately, by using the 🖾 (**Insert Microsoft Excel Worksheet**) button on the standard toolbar. When you click on this button a drop-down list appears so that you can choose the size of the worksheet. This is not critical, as the size of the worksheet can be altered later. The worksheet appears as an object in the document.

Data and formulae can be added as if you were in Excel and while this object is active the toolbars give you access to Excel's functions and commands. When you have completed the worksheet, click outside it to insert it into the document. It looks like a normal Word table but unlike a table it can only be edited by double-clicking on it to open the Excel workspace. Features such as font size, borders and shading can be applied to make the table's presentation and layout consistent with the rest of the document.

By sizing the worksheet area – using the sizing handles – you can control what is embedded in the document so that not all the data in the worksheet need appear. You can also add extra sheets but their data will be hidden unless you display a particular sheet before embedding the worksheet. If you share the document electronically then the underlying data and sheets become accessible when the embedded worksheet is opened.

Task 1: Inserting an Excel spreadsheet

Although Word allows you to do calculations in tables, if you want to perform some repetitive calculations then Excel's **Fill** function is useful. The use of this function is illustrated in this task.

1. Create the following document and save it as *Sales*. Select the table and copy it. Click on a blank line below the table.

	Vendor	Value	Completion Date
56 Bodmin Drive	Mrs J Kettin	56000	4/12/2000
187 Dairyground Road	Dr S Brown	100000	16/12/2000
16 Park Road	Mrs M Lingert	96000	2/1/2001
158 Moss Lane	Mr S Smart	81000	15/1/2001
15 Pownall Avenue	Mrs S Christie	189000	17/1/2001
3 Bude Close	Mr C Shuttle	70000	1/2/2001
2 Woodford Close	Mr M Singh	150000	3/2/2001
16 The Close	Mr R Nettleton	39000	14/2/2001
	Totals Sales Value		
	Average Sales Value		

2. Click on the **Insert Microsoft Excel Worksheet** button and choose a 4 x 5 grid. Paste in the data you have copied to the clipboard. Adjust the column widths and row height. Use **Format-Cells** to adjust the date formatting. Expand the sheet so you can see the whole table.

	A	B	C	D
1		Vendor	Value	Completion Date
2	56 Bodmin Drive	Mrs J Kettin	56000	4-Dec-00
3	187 Dairyground Road	Dr S Brown	100000	16-Dec-00
4	16 Park Road	Mrs M Lingert	96000	2-Jan-01
5	158 Moss Lane	Mr S Smart	81000	15-Jan-01
6	15 Pownall Avenue	Mrs S Christie	189000	17-Jan-01
7	3 Bude Close	Mr C Shuttle	70000	1-Feb-01
8	2 Woodford Close	Mr M Singh	150000	3-Feb-01
9	16 The Close	Mr R Nettleton	39000	14-Feb-01
10		**Totals Sales**		
11		**Average Sales**		

Sheet1

3. Click in the document to embed the worksheet.

4. Double-click on the embedded worksheet to edit it. Add formulae for the total and average. Apply suitable changes to the number format. Embed the worksheet to see the result.

	A	B	C	D
1		Vendor	Value	Completion Date
2	56 Bodmin Drive	Mrs J Kettin	56,000	4-Dec-00
3	187 Dairyground Road	Dr S Brown	100,000	16-Dec-00
4	16 Park Road	Mrs M Lingert	96,000	2-Jan-01
5	158 Moss Lane	Mr S Smart	81,000	15-Jan-01
6	15 Pownall Avenue	Mrs S Christie	189,000	17-Jan-01
7	3 Bude Close	Mr C Shuttle	70,000	1-Feb-01
8	2 Woodford Close	Mr M Singh	150,000	3-Feb-01
9	16 The Close	Mr R Nettleton	39,000	14-Feb-01
10		**Totals Sales**	781,000	
11		**Average Sales**	97,625	

Sheet1

5. Double-click on the worksheet, select column D and choose **Insert-Columns**. Add the following data to this column:

> Registration date
>
> 3-Nov-2000
>
> 6-Jun-2001
>
> 4-Feb-2001
>
> 20-Oct-2001
>
> 14-Sep-2001

13-Aug-2001

6-Nov-2001

25-Nov-2001

6. Widen the worksheet space by dragging on its sizing handle. In cell F2 add the formula **=(E2-D2)/7** to calculate the number of weeks the properties have been on the books. Format this cell as an integer.

7. Select cells F2 to F9 and use **Edit-Fill-Down** to fill the empty cells. Embed the worksheet and save.

	A	B	C	D	E	F
1		Vendor	Value	Registration Date	Completion Date	No. weeks
2	56 Bodmin Drive	Mrs J Kettin	56,000	3-Nov-00	4-Dec-00	4
3	187 Dairyground Road	Dr S Brown	100,000	6-Jun-00	16-Dec-00	28
4	16 Park Road	Mrs M Lingert	96,000	4-Feb-00	2-Jan-01	48
5	158 Moss Lane	Mr S Smart	81,000	20-Oct-00	15-Jan-01	12
6	15 Pownall Avenue	Mrs S Christie	189,000	24-Sep-00	17-Jan-01	16
7	3 Bude Close	Mr C Shuttle	70,000	13-Aug-00	1-Feb-01	25
8	2 Woodford Close	Mr M Singh	150,000	6-Nov-00	3-Feb-01	13
9	16 The Close	Mr R Nettleton	39,000	25-Nov-00	14-Feb-01	12
10		Totals Sales	781,000			
11		Average Sales	97,625			

Sheet1

Creating a PowerPoint presentation from a Word outline

You can use an existing Word document to create a PowerPoint presentation. To set up the slides in a presentation, PowerPoint uses the heading styles in your Word document. For example, each paragraph formatted with the *Heading 1* style becomes the title of a new slide, each *Heading 2* becomes the first level of text, and so on.

To create a PowerPoint presentation from a Word document:

1. Open the document from which you want to create a PowerPoint presentation.

2. Choose **File-Send To** and then select **Microsoft PowerPoint**.

If you're already working in PowerPoint, you can import a Word document into PowerPoint. In PowerPoint, choose **File-Open** and in the **Files of type** box, select **All Outlines**. In the **File name** box, enter the filename and location of the Word document.

You can also insert slides from a Word outline into an existing presentation. In PowerPoint, display the slide after which you want to insert the new slides. Choose **Insert-Slides from Outline**, and then select the Word document.

Task 2: Creating a slide presentation from a Word outline

For this task you will need both Word and PowerPoint.

1. Open the document *Letting*, choose **File-Send To** and then select **Microsoft PowerPoint**.

2. PowerPoint opens in Outline view, showing the headings from this document.

A Guide to Letting your Home

- **Deciding whether to let or sell**

- **Professionals who care**

- **How much will it cost?**

- **Do I have to pay tax on the rent I receive?**

- **Need to know more?**

- **Decided to sell?**

---

3. Experiment with changing the heading levels in this outline, using the **Promote** and **Demote** buttons. You will have to promote several headings to the top level to give you more slides.

4. You can also add and delete text to complete the slide show. To see how to apply formatting, design and other effects, refer to *PowerPoint Basic Skills*.

5. If you want to save the PowerPoint formatting, save the presentation.

Linking and embedding

Information can be shared between Office applications by using linked and embedded objects. Information from other applications that support object linking and embedding can also be shared. If the information you want to use was created in an application that does not support linked and embedded objects, you can still copy and paste information from the file created by that application, to share the information between programs.

The main differences between linked objects and embedded objects are where the data is stored and how it is updated after you place it in the destination file.

❑ With a linked object, information is updated only if you modify the source file. Linked data is stored in the source file. The destination file stores only the location of the source file and displays a representation of the linked data. Use linked objects if file size is a consideration.

❑ With an embedded object, information in the destination file does not change if you modify the source file. Embedded objects become part of the destination file and, once inserted, are no longer part of the source file. Double-click the embedded object to open it in the source program.

Task 3: Linking Word and Excel

For this task you will need both Word and Excel. In Task 1 you have already seen how to embed a worksheet in Word; if you are entering new data then this is probably the best way to handle it. On the other hand, data may be already available in Excel and you may wish to link it to a document so that it can be kept up-to-date. To illustrate this we will copy and paste the data from Task 1 into Excel.

1. Open the document *Sales*, created in Task 1 and double-click on the embedded worksheet. Select the data and copy it. Start Excel and paste the data into a new worksheet. Reinstate the formulae. Save the worksheet as *Sales*.

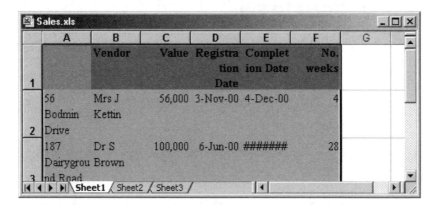

2. Now copy the data from the spreadsheet and open a new document in Word. Choose **Edit-Paste Special**, choose **Microsoft Excel Worksheet Object**, click on

Paste Link and click on **OK**. A table of data will be pasted into the document (this will need reformatting).

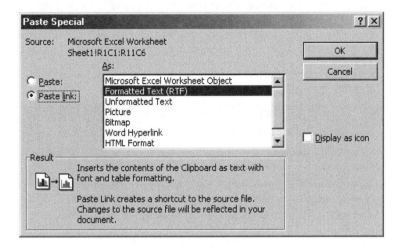

3. Return to Excel and make some changes to the dates. Display Word again and note that the changes made are reflected in the Word document. Do not save the Word document or the changes to the Excel worksheet *Sales*.

Task 4: Linking Word and PowerPoint

For this task you will need both Word and PowerPoint.

1. Open the document *Sales*, select and copy the data in the original Word table.

2. Start PowerPoint, choosing a new presentation and select a blank slide.

3. Choose **Edit-Paste Special**, choose **Paste Link** and click on **OK**.

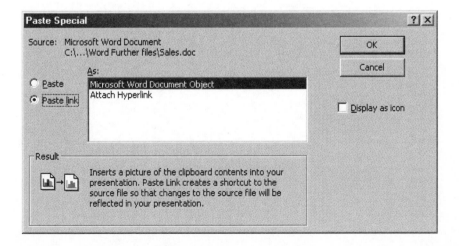

4. The table of data will be pasted into the slide. Drag to resize the table.

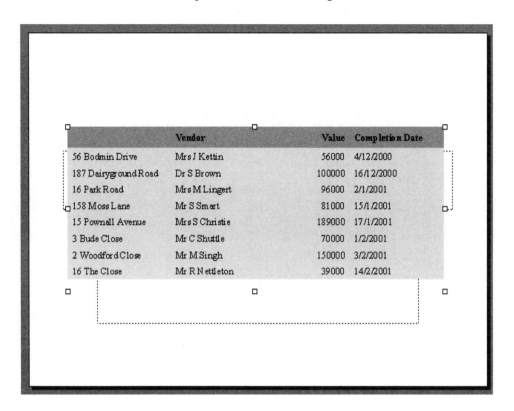

5. Return to Word and make some changes to the text in the table. Display PowerPoint again and note that the changes made are reflected in the table in the slide. Do not save the PowerPoint presentation or the changes to *Sales*.

Using WordArt

What you will learn in this unit

WordArt allows you to form interesting designs and graphics based on text, such as signs and logos. You can use WordArt for any application in which you wish to use text to draw attention an area of a document or leave an image in the memory of the user. Often WordArt is used alongside some other graphical image.

At the end of this unit you will be able to:

❑ Select a WordArt style.

❑ Move, delete and edit WordArt.

❑ Format WordArt, using the WordArt toolbar.

Selecting a WordArt style

Creating a basic WordArt object is very straightforward. Once this object has been created, it is possible either to use it as it is or to apply some of the more ambitious formatting that is available through the WordArt toolbar. Remember to work in Page Layout view throughout this unit.

Create a basic WordArt object as follows:

1. Click on **Insert-Picture-WordArt**. The WordArt Style dialog box is displayed. Choose a style from those that are displayed.

2. Click on **OK**. The WordArt Text dialog box appears.

3. Type in your text. Set font size, and whether bold or italic formatting should be applied. Click on **OK**.

4. The WordArt is inserted in your document.

Task 1: Creating a basic WordArt object

This task creates a small document using the text below.

1. Click on **Insert-Picture-WordArt**. The WordArt Style dialog box is displayed. Choose a style from those that are displayed: for example, the style in the first row, fourth column.

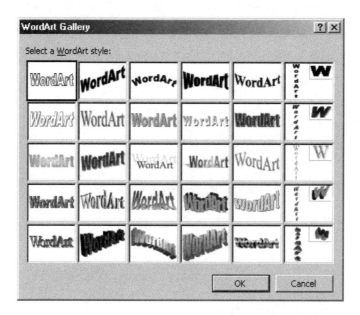

2. Click on **OK**. The WordArt Text dialog box appears.

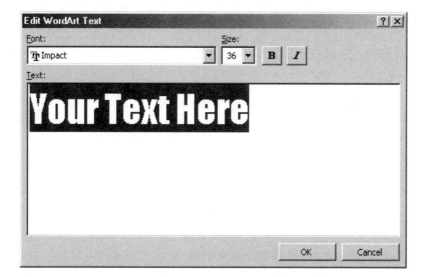

3. Type in 'For Sale'. Choose a font size, say 32 point. Click on **OK**.

4. The WordArt will be inserted in your document. Do not panic if the WordArt is not positioned in an appropriate place in your document. Save the file as *For Sale*.

Moving, deleting and editing WordArt

WordArt seems to have a mind of its own when selecting where to place itself in a document. If you are creating a new piece of WordArt from scratch, it will normally be inserted somewhere close to the insertion point, but if you are cutting and pasting WordArt from another document (which is quite common practice, since you will probably wish to re-use these images) then it seems that there is no knowing where the WordArt will position itself. It may even take up a position in the middle of your text and trigger text wrapping.

To move WordArt, simply move the mouse pointer over the WordArt until the pointer becomes a cross. Then click and drag the object to the desired position. Once selected, fine positioning of the Word Art image can be achieved using the arrow keys on the keyboard.

Alternatively, WordArt can be moved between documents and between pages within documents by using the normal cut-and-paste or copy-and-paste routines.

To edit WordArt, a single click on the WordArt, will bring up the WordArt toolbar; the functions of the buttons on this toolbar are described below.

A double-click will recall the Edit WordArt Text dialog box, which allows you to change text and font size and choose whether bold or italic is applied.

To delete WordArt:

1. WordArt is selected when it has white boxes or handles displayed (like other floating objects that you will have encountered in Word). When initially inserted in the document, these will be displayed. Otherwise, click on the WordArt to select it; the handles are displayed.

2. Press the *Delete* key.

Task 2: Editing WordArt

1. Open the *For Sale* file that you created in Task 1. Click on the WordArt to select it.

2. Choose **Edit-Copy**, move the insertion point down the page and choose **Edit-Paste**.

3. Double-click on the copy of the WordArt to display the Edit WordArt Text dialog box.

4. Edit the text to read *For Sale/To Let*.

5. Click on **OK** to insert the new WordArt in your document.

6. The WordArt will probably appear squashed. Using the selection handles stretch it until the text can be read more clearly.

Task 3: Using the WordArt toolbar

Once you have created a piece of WordArt, the tools on the WordArt toolbar can be used to create a range of different effects. The table below shows some of the effects that can be created by clicking on the different buttons on the toolbar. Take a piece of WordArt that you have created and try to replicate the effects in this table. You may also like to experiment with the use of colours. Logos and other applications of WordArt are often the main application for colours on standard documents.

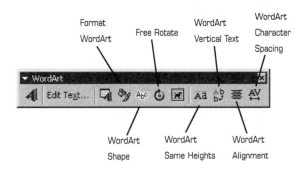

Button	Example
Format WordArt	For sale
WordArt Shape	For sale
Free Rotate	For sale

Button	Example
WordArt Same Heights	**For sale**
WordArt Vertical Text	**For sale** (vertical)
WordArt Alignment	**For sale**
WordArt Character Spacing	**For s a le**

Task 4: Using WordArt in a poster

One common application for WordArt is in the context of posters and other displays. This task demonstrates how WordArt can be used to effect on a hand bill or small poster.

Create the price list below. Insert WordArt at the top and bottom of the page, so that the finished work looks like the example below.

1. Type in the text and save it as *Price List*. Choose **Insert-Picture-WordArt**.

2. Choose a shape from the WordArt Gallery.

3. Type in the text 'Bishop's Place' and adjust its size to around 60 points (so that it will fill the width of the page).

4. Choose a shape using the shape tool on the WordArt toolbar, for example, **Can Up**.

5. Stretch the WordArt to fill the width of the page and, if necessary, move the WordArt into position at the top of the page. You may wish to set text wrapping to **Top** and **Bottom**.

Bishop's Place

Development	**Bishop's Place, Eyebrook Road, Bowdon**
Sales Negotiator	**Ann Dilorenzo**
Telephone No	**0161-926-9392**

Sales Office Opening Hours Open 7 days 10am-5pm

Plot No	House Type and Accommodation	Completion Date	Sales Price
3	5 bed detached with double garage	February 2002	£322,500
4	5 bed detached with double garage	February 2002	£327,500
5	5 bed detached with double garage	March 2002	£325,000
6	5 bed detached with triple garage with games room over	March 2002	£355,950

SHOW HOME: PLOT 2

Sold

RESERVATION DEPOSIT: £300   TENURE: FREEHOLD

Completion Dates:	These are for guidance only, and our Sales Negotiator will keep you advised of any variations.
Sales Price:	These particulars are subject to contract and availability at the time of mailing. We would recommend you contact our Sales Office as soon as possible.

Bishop's Place

6. Now, to create the WordArt at the bottom of the page select the existing WordArt, choose **Edit-Copy** and then **Edit-Paste**.

7. Move the new copy of WordArt to the bottom of the page.

8. Using the shape tool on the WordArt toolbar select an appropriate shape for this copy of the WordArt. You now have similar but differently-shaped WordArt at the top and bottom of the page.

9. Add the *Sold* tag using WordArt and a rectangle. Add the WordArt and draw a rectangle around it (you may need to 'send the rectangle to the back' to stop it obscuring the WordArt). Group the two objects and use the rotate tool to tilt the grouped object.

Creating WordArt as an in-line image

As you have seen in this unit, WordArt is by default a floating image. You cannot change it into an in-line image using the **Position** tab in the **Format-Object** dialog box as the **Float over text** check box is not available.

To create WordArt as an in-line image, first open a picture workspace, using **Insert-Object-Microsoft Word Picture**. Create the WordArt as described in this unit for normal WordArt, click on the **Reset Picture Boundary** button in the Edit-Picture toolbar and the **Close Picture** button to insert the picture into your document. This 'picture' of the WordArt can be formatted as an in-line image. Also, if you want to change your document to HTML format (see Unit 17) then WordArt that has been created inside a picture object will be converted to a Web graphics file.

Using Graph

What you will learn in this unit

This unit covers the basic functions necessary to create and save charts. The data to be displayed in the chart is entered in a datasheet. By entering text in the top row and the first column it is possible to add labels to the chart. In addition, formatting data on the datasheet can affect the formatting of data elsewhere.

The next unit explores the variety of different ways in which you can format charts.

At the end of this unit you will be able to:

❑ Start Word's charting facility, Microsoft Graph.

❑ Enter data into a datasheet.

❑ Create a chart and embed it into a Word document.

❑ Edit and print a chart.

❑ Move around the datasheet.

❑ Edit the values in cells and change column widths.

❑ Clear, move and copy data, and insert and delete rows and columns.

❑ Define the data series to be displayed.

Microsoft Graph

To start Graph, with a Word document open choose **Insert-Object-Microsoft Graph 2000 Chart** or click the ▥ (**Insert Chart**) button on the toolbar. If this button is not shown on your toolbar then you may have to add it (see *Customising toolbars* in the Appendix). The screen will display a linked datasheet and chart which may show the default chart. Data entered on the datasheet is displayed on the chart.

The Datasheet window

The Datasheet window is like a simple spreadsheet worksheet. Labels for data are entered in the first row and column of the datasheet. Do not type data in these cells. This first row and column remain visible as you scroll through the sheet.

Document1 - Datasheet			A	B	C	D	E
			1st Qtr	2nd Qtr	3rd Qtr	4th Qtr	
1		East	20.4	27.4	90	20.4	
2		West	30.6	38.6	34.6	31.6	
3		North	45.9	46.9	45	43.9	
4							

Various parts of the datasheet have names that are used later. The important components of the datasheet are listed in the following table:

Component	Description
Row and column headings	Above the first row and to the left of the first column of the datasheet
Cell	One rectangle of the datasheet
Active cell	Currently selected cell
Data point	Single cell value
Data series	A row or column of data used to plot one set of bars or columns, a line or a pie chart.
Series names	Names that identify each row and column of data
Tick mark labels	When the data series are in rows, the tick mark labels are the column labels; when data series are in columns, the tick mark labels are the row labels

The chart

The data appears in the document in the form of a chart. Again, parts of the window have names that will be used later.

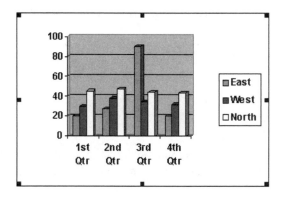

The important components of the chart window are listed in the following table:

Component	Description
Chart	The entire area inside the chart window
Data marker	A bar, shape or dot that marks a single data point or value
Data series	A group of related data points
Axis	A line that serves as a reference for plotting data on a chart
Tick mark	A small line that intersects the axis and marks off a category
Plot area	The area in which Graph plots the data
Gridlines	Lines that extend from the tick marks across the chart
Chart text	Text that describes data or items in a chart
Legend	The key

Managing the Datasheet window and chart

All of the operations that can normally be performed on windows can be performed on the Datasheet window. It can be sized by moving its borders, or moved by dragging the title bar to a new position.

To switch between windows, click on the one that you wish to be active. If you would like to remove the Datasheet window, click on **View-Datasheet**. The Datasheet can be recalled by applying **View-Datasheet** again. Alternatively, click on the (**View-Datasheet**) button on the toolbar.

Creating a simple chart

To create a simple chart you merely need to enter data into the datasheet. If you already have the default data and chart on your screen, you will first need to clear the default data. This can be achieved as follows:

1. Select the datasheet, by clicking in the top left-hand box. The datasheet should be highlighted in black.

2. Press the *Delete* key.

3. Click on any datasheet cell to clear the highlight.

Once you have an empty datasheet and chart you are ready to begin. Enter labels in the first row and first column and data in the remaining cells. Move from one cell to the next by using the *Tab* or right arrow key. To move backwards from one cell to another use *Shift-Tab* or the left arrow key. Use the up and down arrow keys to move the active cell up or down. You may also use the mouse pointer to position the active cell by pointing and clicking.

Inserting a chart into a document

To insert a chart into a document, simply click on the document outside the chart. The hatching border will disappear. Once in the document the chart may be selected and manipulated with any of the operations that can be applied to any other 'floating' object, such as moving, copying, cutting, pasting and sizing. If you do not want the chart to 'float' (and note that floating objects do not appear in Normal view) then with the chart selected use **Format-Object**, choose the **Layout** tab and select one of the options other than **In line with text**.

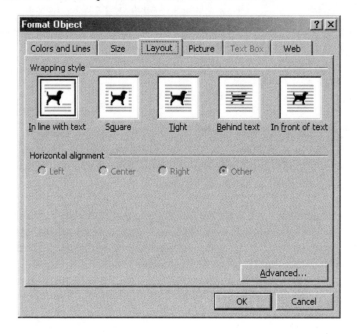

Saving a chart

Charts are saved as part of the document in which they are embedded. To save a chart, place the chart in a document and save the document in the normal way using **File-Save**. Note that the chart, the data and all formats are saved as part of your document.

Printing a chart

Charts are also printed as part of the document in which they are embedded. Print the document in the normal way using **File-Print Preview** to view the document first and then click on the ⊜ button.

Editing a chart

To edit a chart:

1. Double-click on the chart in your document.

2. Make whatever changes you wish to the chart or the data.

3. When finished click on the main document and save.

Task 1: Creating a chart of one data series

This task creates a simple chart showing one data series, as shown below. The chart illustrates the number of property sales for each price range during October.

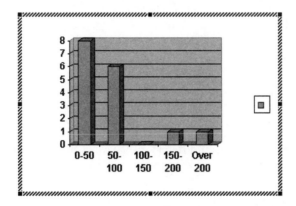

1. Start a new document. Choose **Insert-Object-Microsoft Graph 2000 Chart** or click on ▥ (**Insert Chart**) to start Graph. The default datasheet and chart should be displayed.

2. If necessary clear the default chart as indicated above.

3. Enter the labels in the first row and the data in the second row, leaving the first column blank. Note that at this point you cannot see the full labels in the first row.

		A	B	C	D	E	
		0-50	50-100	100-150	150-200	Over 200	
1	3-D Colum	8	6	0	1	1	
2							
3							
4							

Document1 - Datasheet

4. Move the Datasheet window to examine your chart. It may not be exactly like the one illustrated; any further formatting will be done later.

5. Insert the chart in the document by clicking outside it.

6. Use **File-Save** to save the document, with its embedded chart, using the filename *Property Sales*.

Creating two or more copies of a chart

Once you have inserted a chart into a document you may create an additional copy by cutting and pasting.

1. Select the chart.

2. Choose **Edit-Copy**.

3. Move the insertion point to where you wish to insert the second copy of the chart in your document.

4. Choose **Edit-Paste**.

This operation can also be used to transfer charts between documents, if you have two or more documents open in separate windows.

A copy of the chart may be edited and used to create another chart based on the same or related data. Thus several different displays can be created showing the same or different subsets of a single data series.

Task 2: Creating a chart with two data series

The objective of this task is to create two copies of a chart, and then to reformat the second chart.

1. Select your chart in the document *Property Sales* by clicking on it.

2. Make a second copy using **Edit-Copy**, move the cursor to the position for the second copy and use **Edit-Paste**. (You may need to press *Enter* a few times to create some space.)

3. Double-click on the second chart to start Graph. If the Datasheet window is not active, click on it.

4. Add the data for the next two rows in the datasheet.

Property Sales.doc - Datasheet		A	B	C	D	E	
		0-50	50-100	100-150	150-200	Over 200	
1	3-D Colum	8	6	0	1	1	
2	3-D Colum	6	7	3	0	0	
3	3-D Colum	5	3	2	1	0	
4							

5. Examine the new chart. Two data series should now be displayed as below. Drag the sizing handle of the chart to make it fit across the width of the page.

6. Update the chart in the document. Do not worry if your chart does not look exactly like the one illustrated; chart formatting is discussed in Unit 12. Note that you now have two versions of your chart in your document. Save the document again.

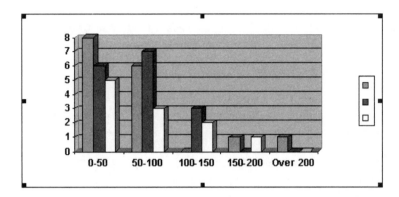

Working with datasheets

The following table summarises some of the key datasheet operations:

To	Do this
Select a cell	Click on the cell.
Select a range of cells	Point to the first cell, and drag through the remaining cells.
Select a row or column	Click on the grey box at the side of a row or at the top of a column.
Select an entire datasheet	Click on the grey box in the upper left corner of the datasheet.
Enter data	Select cell, type data and press *Enter*.
Edit data	Double-click on cells so that the insertion point appears in the cell. Position insertion point and edit.
Clear cell contents	Select cells. Either press the *Delete* key or choose **Edit-Clear**. Decide whether you wish to clear **All**, **Formats** or **Contents**.
Undo changes	Choose **Edit-Undo**.
Change column widths	Move the pointer onto the top of the column boundary until it appears as a double-headed arrow. Drag the line to the right of the column heading to give the required width.

Insert a row or column	Select row or columns where the new row or column is to go. Choose **Insert-Cells**.
Delete a row or column	Select the row or column to be deleted. Choose **Edit-Delete**.
Move data	Select cells. Choose **Edit-Cut**. Select upper left cell of paste area. Choose **Edit-Paste**.
Copy data	Select cells. Choose **Edit-Copy**. Select upper left cell of paste area. Choose **Edit-Paste**.

Task 3: Formatting and editing a datasheet

Using the second chart in the document *Property Sales*, you can improve the format of the datasheet so that it appears similar to the one displayed below. Here are some functions to try.

1. If necessary, widen the columns so that the labels in the first row can be displayed clearly, by placing the pointer on the column boundary and dragging the column line to the right of the desired column heading to give an appropriate width.

2. Enter **October, November** and **December** in the first column against the respective rows of data.

3. Enter additional data for the following three months in the next three rows, as shown.

Property Sales.doc - Datasheet

		A 0-50	B 50-100	C 100-150	D 150-200	E Over 200
1	October	8	6	0	1	1
2	November	6	7	3	0	0
3	December	5	3	2	1	0
4	January	4	2	2	0	0
5	February	3	2	1	0	1
6	March	9	6	4	1	0
7						

4. Insert a new column to the left of the *0-50* column to accommodate the following data by clicking on the column A heading and using **Insert-Cells**. Widen the column as necessary to accommodate the heading.

    Total   16   16   11   8   6   20

5. Move the column with the *Total* heading to the right of the *Over 200* column. Select the cells in the *Total* column and then put them on the clipboard using **Edit-Cut**. Next click on the top cell in the new empty column and choose **Edit-Paste**. Delete the empty column A.

6. Your datasheet should now show the following data:

		A	B	C	D	E	F	
		0-50	50-100	100-150	150-200	Over 200	Total	
1	October	8	6	0	1	1	16	
2	November	6	7	3	0	0	16	
3	December	5	3	2	1	0	11	
4	January	4	2	2	0	0	8	
5	February	3	2	1	0	1	6	
6	March	9	6	4	1	0	20	
7								

Property Sales.doc - Datasheet

7. Examine your chart. It is now attempting to display too much data and does not look very effective. You need to choose which data to display. For now, simply click anywhere in your document and save it again.

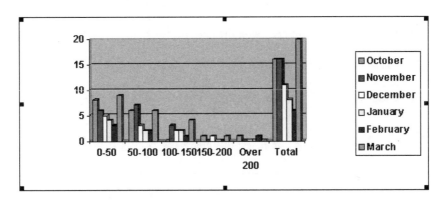

Determining which data is displayed on the chart

In your first chart design you will have accepted the default arrangement, which is that all data on the datasheet is displayed on the chart, and each row is regarded as one data series. Often you may wish to be more selective and display only some of the data in one chart, and other data on a later chart. Graph has commands that are useful in this context:

❏ The **Data** menu offers the opportunity to define which sets of data should by displayed as a data series. Two important options that determine which way you look at the data are **Data-Series in Columns** and **Data-Series in Rows**.

❏ Excluding and including data: these options control the data that will appear on the chart, so that data may remain on the datasheet but need not appear on the chart. To exclude data, select a row or column. Choose **Data-Exclude Row/Col**. Note that the excluded data row or column is no longer displayed on the chart, and appears dimmed on the datasheet and that the heading cell for excluded columns or rows loses its 'button-like' appearance.

A quicker method of excluding is to double-click the row heading to the left of the row or the column heading above the column.

Once excluded, rows or columns can be included again by a similar process.

Task 4: Creating a series of charts from a single chart

This task again uses the chart and datasheet that you have embedded in the document *Property Sales*. Open the document and click on the last chart. The chart is currently showing too many data series to be effective, so you will have to be more selective and create a series of charts that show selected data series. Suppose, for example, that you wish to compare the sales for the first and last months shown. Alternatively, you might like to compare *0-50* data with *50-100* data. You can create two charts to display such data.

To create a chart comparing the first and last months, double-click on the chart that you have been working with to display its datasheet.

1. Select the middle four rows on the datasheet.

2. Choose **Data-Exclude Row/Col**.

3. Examine the chart, which should now only show the data for the first and last months.

4. Click in the document to insert this chart.

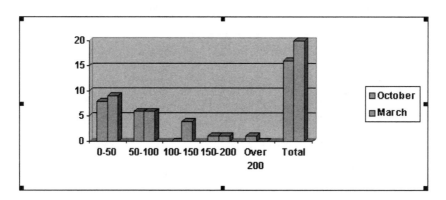

5. You can now create a chart comparing *0-50* data with *50-100* data. To create other charts based on the same datasheet, create an additional copy of the chart using **Edit-Copy** and **Edit-Paste**.

6. Double-click on the new copy of the chart to load Graph again and display the datasheet once more.

7. Include the excluded rows, using **Data-Include Row/Col**.

8. Exclude all columns that you do not wish to display in this chart using **Data-Exclude Row/Col**.

9. Examine the chart, which should now simply compare the data for *0-50* data with that for *50-100*.

10. Insert this chart in the document. Save the document.

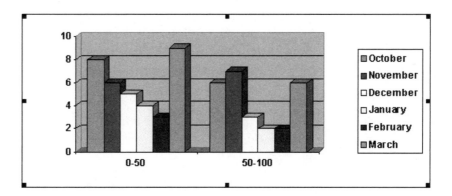

Formatting cells

The appearance of cells in the datasheet can be changed by modifying font, size, style and the colour of data in a cell. There are a number of numerical formats that can be adopted, for example, currency signs, different numbers of decimal places and thousands separators. Numerical values next to tick marks can be changed by defining or changing the number format of the cell in the second column of the second row of the datasheet. All of the formatting options are shown on the Format menu.

Task 5: Formatting cells

Using the datasheet associated with the *Property Sales* chart, experiment with formatting the cells, using the options on the **Format** menu. For example, you might try the following:

1. Using **Format-Font** to change the font and size of the text.

2. Using **Format-Number** to choose different formats for the data. Do not save your changes.

Formatting Charts

What you will learn in this unit

Graph offers a number of different means for formatting charts. This unit explores some of the options by indicating possible chart types and formatting options. Charts need to be clearly labelled. Some text is placed on the chart by Graph. You can also delete or edit this text and add other text. Typically text on a chart includes chart titles, axes labels, data marker labels and other text.

Text can be attached or unattached. Typical *attached* text includes chart titles, axes labels and data marker labels. *Unattached* text may be moved freely to any position on the chart.

Other features of charts that can be manipulated and changed include gridlines, arrows, legend (key), axis, data chart markers and data marker patterns.

At the end of this unit you will be able to:

❏   Select a chart type, such as bar, area or column.

❏   Select a chart format, such as the type of bar or pie chart.

❏   Add attached and unattached text.

❏   Select, edit, delete or move text.

❏   Change text font, alignment and orientation.

❏   Format axes and gridlines.

❏   Add, place and format the legend.

❏   Insert data labels.

What you need

To complete this unit you will need:

❏   The document file *Property Sales* created in Unit 11.

Chart types

To date we have used the default chart format, which is the column chart. To explore other formats that are available, use **Chart-Chart Type** and select a chart type.

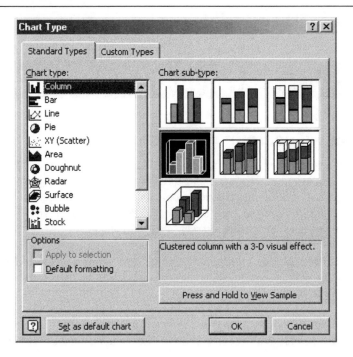

Options include: bar, area, column, line, pie, combination, XY scatter, 3-D area, 3-D bar, 3-D column, 3-D pie and 3-D line. These are listed in the **Chart Type** dialog box. The **Custom Type** tab offers some further options.

 Note: It is important to choose chart type first as any subsequent formatting applies to a specific chart type.

Task 1: Using chart type

Using the *Property Sales* chart, experiment with displaying the data in different formats and chart types, by investigating the options under **Chart Type**. Note that some chart types are more suitable than others for your data. Good charts are charts that suit their purpose. To add data labels as illustrated, select **Chart-Chart Options** and click on the **Data Labels** tab. Select **Show value**. Do not save these changes.

Hints for good charts

Since there is a wide range of different chart types available the most difficult decision is the choice of the correct chart type to display a specific data series effectively. To some extent this is a matter of personal preference, but the set of hints below offers some general guidelines that you may wish to consider:

1. Think about the appearance of the chart when it is printed on paper. It is easy to get carried away when you are designing a chart on a coloured screen. Think about whether the data series that are shown will be sufficiently differentiated when printed on a non-colour printer. Test this.

2. Do not display too many data series on one chart; three is often sufficient.

3. When using bar or column charts distinguish between when composite and normal bar or column charts are appropriate. Think about which data you are comparing with which other data.

4. Use 3-D charts sparingly. Only simple 3-D charts look effective on paper.

5. Only use pie charts to display parts of a whole. It is inadvisable to explode more than one segment. The format that is often most helpful shows data labels and percentages.

6. Use line graphs to join distinct data points. Use different data markers to denote different data series.

7. Check that the chart has a title, axes, labels, data and, when more than one data series is displayed, a legend.

8. Try not to cover data markers with text such as titles or the legend. If necessary move text and legend.

9. Examine the chart for legibility. Turn the tick mark labels round or change their size if necessary.

10. Remember that the most effective charts often show a very limited set of data, effectively labelled.

11. Only use gridlines sparingly.

12. When creating a number of charts in a document, try to develop a style so that comparable data appears on a similarly formatted chart.

Working with chart text

The following table summarises the key operations that you may wish to perform on chart text:

To	Do this
Add attached text	Choose **Chart-Chart Options-Titles**. Select the appropriate part of the chart to which you wish to add text. Type in text. Click on **OK**. The text appears in black selection squares. Press *Esc*.
Add unattached text	Type the text required. The text appears in black squares indicating that you can move and size the text. Press *Esc*. This text is in a text box.
Select text	Click on the text.

To	Do this
Edit text	Select text, then retype it, or position the insertion point within the text and insert or delete characters. Press *Esc*.
Delete text	Select text, and press the *Delete* key.
Move unattached text	Select text to show the border surrounding the text, drag to the position that you want.
Display data labels, values or percentages	Switch to Chart window. Choose **Chart-Chart Options** and select appropriate options. Click on **OK**.

The chart text font, alignment and orientation can be changed. In addition it is possible to change the pattern and colour of the text area and the colour, weight and style of the border around the text. To illustrate this process, consider changing the orientation of axis labels on the x-axis from horizontal to vertical.

1. Select the axis.

2. The name of the selected component will appear in the box on the toolbar.

3. The text can be formatted using either the buttons on the toolbar or using **Format-Font** or **Format-Selected Axis**.

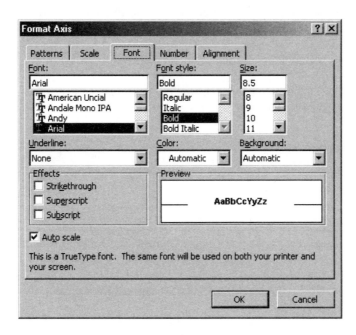

4. Experiment with setting different fonts and text alignments, using both toolbar buttons and the wider range of options offered through the dialog boxes.

Task 2: Adding labels and headings

This task adds some axis labels and a title to the chart and investigates other formatting that might be necessary. In the document *Property Sales*, use the chart that compares *0-50* data with *50-100* data. You can add some labels to this, so that it starts to look like the chart below.

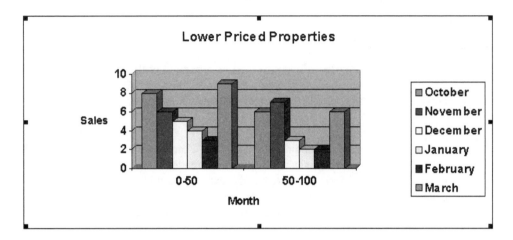

1. Double-click on the chart to load Graph. Click on the chart to select it.

2. Choose **Chart-Chart Options** and select the **Titles** tab. Type the title – e.g. *Lower Priced Properties* – in the **Chart title** box. Click on **OK**. This appears in black selection squares. To remove these squares, press *Esc*.

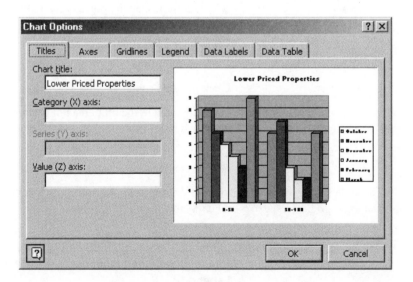

3. Choose **Chart-Chart Options**. Type in the text – e.g. *Month* – in the **Category (X) axis** box. This appears in black selection squares.

4. Type in the text – e.g. *Sales* – in the **Value (Z) axis** box. Click on **OK**.

5. You will observe that adding labels tends to shrink the size of the chart display. Stretch the chart to a suitable size, taking care not to exceed the margins.

6. Insert the chart into the document *Property Sales* and save the document.

Chart formatting

Every feature of a chart can be modified or formatted in the same way. Many of the options to perform these operations are under the **Chart Options** menu. First, however, before you can format or edit a chart item, it must be selected.

When a chart item is selected it is marked with either white squares or black squares and a border, depending upon its type. Chart items and text marked with white squares or handles and a border can be formatted with commands and moved or sized with the mouse. Chart items and text marked with only selection squares cannot be moved or sized directly. Some items, such as axis labels, can be formatted or realigned with commands. It is useful to review the means for selecting parts of charts.

To	Do this
Select an item	Click on the item.
Select a series	Click any marker in the series.
Select a single data marker	To format a single data marker, click it once to select the series, again to select the individual marker, and then double-click it to display the Format Data Point dialog box.
Select gridlines	Click on a gridline.
Select axis	Click the area containing the axis tick mark labels.
Select the entire plot area	Click any area in the plot area not occupied by another item.
Select the entire chart	Click anywhere outside the plot area, where there is not another item.

The table below summarises some of the key operations necessary in order to format axes, gridlines, legends and data labels:

To	Do this
Add a legend	Choose **Chart-Chart Options-Legend-Show Legend**.
Delete a legend	Choose **Edit-Clear** or set using **Show Legend** as above.

To	Do this
Move a legend	Drag it to a new position.
Format the border and the legend box	Choose **Format-Selected Legend**. Under the **Patterns** tab, select the border and area options that you want. To format the legend text font, choose the **Font** tab and select the options that you want.
Format gridlines	Select one of the major gridlines for the axis, and choose **Format-Selected Gridlines**. Select the style, colour and weight and choose **OK**.
Show axes labels	Click on **Chart-Chart Options-Axes** and select to display appropriate axes.
Format the axis scale	Click on axis to be formatted. Choose **Format-Selected axis** and choose the **Scale** tab. Enter the appropriate values or select or clear boxes to achieve the scale format required.
Format axis patterns and tick mark label location	Select an axis to be formatted. Choose **Format-Selected axis** and choose the **Patterns** tab. This will cause the Patterns dialog box to be displayed. Under **Axis** select type, style, colour and weight for the axis line. Select the major and minor tick mark types. Under **Tick mark labels**, select the position on the chart where the tick labels are to appear. To format the tick mark label font choose the **Font** tab. To format the orientation of the tick mark labels, choose the **Alignment** tab and select the options that you want. Click on **OK**.
Show data labels	Choose **Chart-Chart Options-Data Labels** and select appropriate labels.
Format data labels	Select data labels to be formatted. Choose **Format-Format Data Labels**. Select the options that you wish to apply to your chart and click on **OK**.
Clear the data labels format	Select the marker and choose **Edit-Clear**. Select the **Clear** option.

Task 3: Exploring further formatting

The objective of this task is to explore some of the formatting features of Graph.

1. Open *Property Sales* and double-click on the chart.

2. Select the title by clicking on it (the border with black selection squares is displayed). Choose **Format-Selected Chart Title** and choose **Font**, then change the format of the text to, say, italic and a larger font size.

3. Select each of the axis labels in turn. Choose **Format-Selected** and change the format of the text using the **Font** tab.

4. Select each of the axes in turn. Choose **Format-Selected Axis** and choose **Patterns**. In the dialog box, change the tick mark type for **Major** to **Cross** and for **Minor** to **None**.

5. Move the legend by first clicking on it to select it and then dragging it to a better position.

6. Exit Graph and in Word display the drawing toolbar using **View-Toolbars-Drawing**. Click on the arrow and insert an arrow onto the graph. Add a text box.

7. Examine your chart in the document and resave the document.

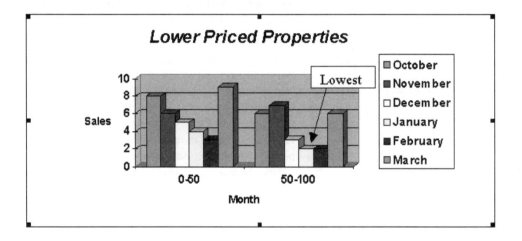

Task 4: Creating a new chart and using it in a document

Create a chart displaying the total sales and properties offered for sale for each month and insert the chart in a document.

		A	B	C	D	E	F
		October	November	December	January	February	March
1	Sales	16	16	11	8	6	20
2	New Properties	12	16	7	11	7	24
3							
4							

1. First create a column chart showing both data series. Do not forget to add axis labels and a title.

2. Format the title and the axis labels appropriately.

3. Format any other features of the chart that you would like to change, such as the axes.

4. Insert the chart into your document.

5. Make a further copy of the chart and use the datasheet associated with this copy to create two more charts.

6. Select each data series in turn – i.e. *Sales* and then *New Properties* – and display each of these on separate bar charts, both of which you should insert into your document.

7. Choose appropriate formatting and check that the axis labels and title are appropriate.

Task 5: Creating a pie chart

Use a pie chart to display the following data concerning the average number of weeks properties remain on the books.

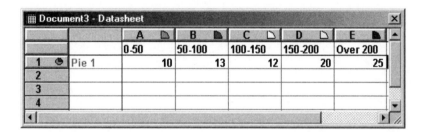

Remember to add a title and experiment with the use of data labels, possibly as percentages. Save this chart in a document called *Average Weeks*.

Creating Macros

What you will learn in this unit

A macro is a series of Word instructions grouped together as a single command to make time-consuming, repetitive tasks easier. You can assign a macro to a toolbar button, a menu item or shortcut keys to make the macro as convenient to use as a built-in Word command. Here are some typical uses for macros:

❏ To speed up routine editing and formatting.

❏ To combine multiple commands.

❏ To make an option in a dialog box more accessible.

❏ To automate a complex series of tasks.

Word offers two methods for creating macros. The first is the macro recorder, which records a set of actions as a series of instructions in Visual Basic for Applications. The second is the Visual Basic Editor, which allows you to code instructions directly. The Visual Basic Editor can also be used to open a recorded macro to modify the instructions. This way you can write very flexible and powerful macros that include Visual Basic instructions that you cannot record using the macro recorder.

After you have assigned a macro to a toolbar button, a menu item or shortcut keys, running the macro is as simple as clicking the toolbar button or menu item or pressing the shortcut keys. You can also choose **Tools-Macro** to run a macro.

You use the Macros dialog box to create, delete or rename a macro. By default, Word stores macros in the Normal template so that they are available for use with every Word document. However, if a macro stored in the Normal template is useful only for a particular type of document, you may want to copy the macro to the template for that type of document and then delete the macro from the Normal template. Macros can be copied using **Format-Style-Organizer** under the **Macro project items** tab.

At the end of this unit you will be able to:

❏ Record and run a simple macro.

❏ Delete a macro.

❏ Assign a macro to a button, a shortcut key and a menu item.

Recording and running a simple macro

Simple macros that automate a repetitive action are easy to record and use. The example that will be considered here is that of applying some specific formatting where certain words within a document will take on this formatting.

Task 1: A simple formatting macro

This task creates a simple macro for applying formatting to one or more characters. This sort of macro is useful for speeding up any tasks that are carried out regularly.

1. Choose **Tools-Macro-Record New Macro**. In the **Macro Name** box type the name of the macro, *RedShadow*, and click on **OK**. Your actions will now be recorded.

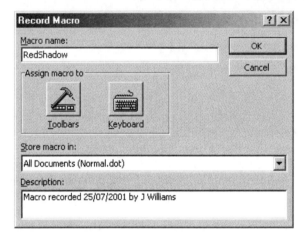

2. Choose **Format-Font** and select the **Shadow** check box and change the colour to red. Click on **OK**. Click on the **Stop Macro** button.

3. To run the macro, select a word in a document, use **Tools-Macro-Macros**, select *RedShadow* from the list (as illustrated below) and click on **Run**.

For such a small amount of formatting this macro is not really saving much time, but if your formatting involved more than this it would be advantageous. By assigning the macro *RedShadow* to a shortcut key the time saving becomes very evident.

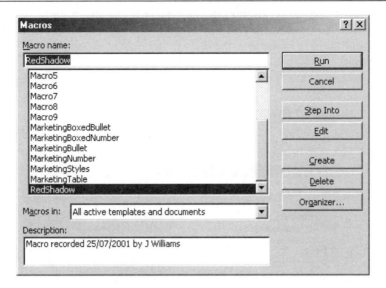

Assigning a macro to a button, shortcut key or menu item

Once a macro has been created it can be run from the Macros dialog box. However, if the macro is to be used often then using **Tools-Macro-Macros** can be time consuming. It is much quicker to run a macro by using a shortcut key or by clicking on a button in one of the toolbars.

When recording a macro you can assign the macro to a shortcut key or a button using the **Keyboard** or **Toolbars** button. If you choose the **Keyboard** button the Customize Keyboard dialog box appears. You can try different keyboard combinations. The **Press new shortcut key** section will tell you whether the shortcut

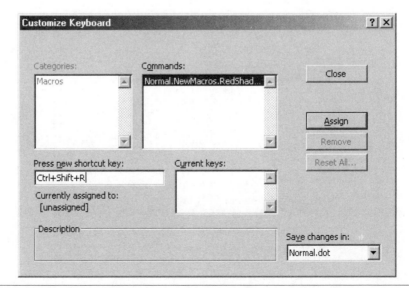

you have chosen has already been assigned to a command. Once you have decided on a shortcut key, click on the **Assign** button and continue to record the macro. When you have recorded it, the shortcut key chosen should run it in future.

If you choose the **Toolbars** button, the Customize dialog box appears.

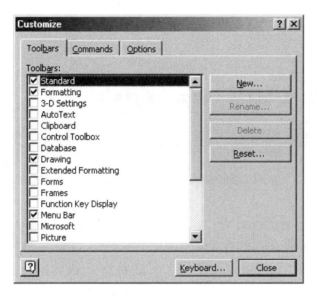

After selecting the **Toolbars** tab, you can add a button to a toolbar as follows:

1. Show the toolbar you want to add a button to (or create a **New** toolbar) and then click the **Commands** tab.

2. The **Macros** line should be highlighted in the **Categories** box.

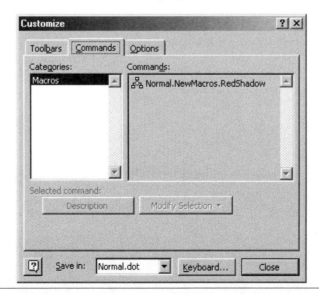

3. Drag the macro you want from the **Commands** box to the displayed toolbar. Click on **Close**.

To add a macro to a menu item usually involves creating a custom menu and then assigning the macro to that menu item. To create a new (custom) menu and add a macro to it:

1. Choose **Tools-Customize**, and select the **Commands** tab.

2. From the **Categories** box, choose **New Menu**.

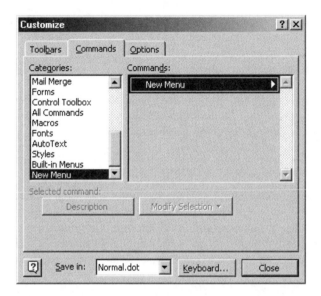

3. Drag **New Menu** from the **Commands** box to the menu bar.

4. Point to **New Menu** on the menu bar, right-click on it and type a name (e.g. *&Macro*) in the **Name** box on the shortcut menu. If you precede a letter in the name with an ampersand (&) then it will be underlined and *Alt* plus the letter will open the menu, but choose a letter not already used by the existing menus. Press *Enter*.

5. To add a command to the new menu, click the menu name on the toolbar to display an empty box. Choose the **Macros** category in the **Categories** box and then drag

the macro from the Commands box to the empty box in the custom menu. Right-click on the new menu item and change the **Name** entry.

Task 2: Assigning a macro to a shortcut key

In this task a macro will be recorded that produces the second of a pair of quotes. Word usually uses 'smart' quotes, i.e. left and right-handed apostrophes that generally occur in pairs. Sometimes, the right-hand apostrophe is needed on its own to indicate an abbreviation. This effect can be achieved by typing two apostrophes and deleting the first. This macro will be recorded and assigned to a shortcut key.

1. Choose **Tools-Macro-Record New Macro** and in the **Macro Name** box type the name of the macro *RHapostrophe* and click on the **Keyboard** button.

2. Choose the keyboard combination *Alt+'* and click on **Assign** and **Close**.

3. You are now ready to record the macro. Use **Insert-Symbol** and choose ' (the right-hand apostrophe). Click on **Insert** and **Close**. Click on the button. This macro will run whenever you use the keyboard shortcut *Alt+'*.

Assigning a shortcut key to an existing macro

You can assign a shortcut to a macro that has already been created:

1. Select **Tools-Customize** and choose the **Commands** tab. Click on the **Keyboard** button. Scroll down the list in the **Categories** and select **Macros**. In the **Commands** box select the macro you wish to assign to a shortcut key.

2. Choose a keyboard combination for the shortcut. Click on **Assign** and then **Close**. Test out the shortcut.

Deleting a macro

To delete a macro:

1. Choose **Tools-Macro-Macros**. In the **Macro name** box, highlight the name of the macro you want to delete by clicking on it.

2. Click on the **Delete** button, reply **Yes** to the message box and click on **Close** to close the dialog box.

If the macro doesn't appear in the **Macro name** box, select a different list of macros from the **Macros in** drop-down list box.

Task 3: Assigning a macro to a menu item

This task places the *RHapostrophe* macro on a custom menu.

1. Choose **Tools-Customize** and select the **Commands** tab. From the **Categories** box, choose **New Menu** and drag **New Menu** from the **Commands** box to the menu bar.

2. Point to **New Menu** on the menu bar and right-click on it. Type the name **&Common** in the **Name** box on the shortcut menu. Press _Enter_.

3. Click on the _Common_ menu name on the toolbar to display an empty box. Choose the **Macro** category in the **Categories** box, select the macro _Normal.NewMacros. RHapostrophe_ and then drag it from the **Commands** box to the empty box in the custom menu. If you right click on this new menu item its name can be edited to read say, **_Right-hand apostrophe_**. Press _Enter_ and close the **Customize** dialog box. Test out the menu and macro.

    Menu items and custom menus may be deleted through the Customize dialog box.

Editing a macro

To edit a macro:

1. Select Tools-Macro-Macros. click on the macro name and then on Edit. The Visual Basic window is displayed, with the macro ready for editing.

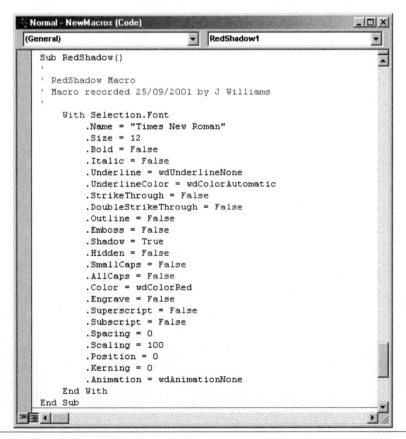

```
Normal - NewMacros (Code)                                    _ □ ×
(General)                              ▼   RedShadow1          ▼
  Sub RedShadow()
  '
  '  RedShadow Macro
  '  Macro recorded 25/09/2001 by J Williams
  '
      With Selection.Font
          .Name = "Times New Roman"
          .Size = 12
          .Bold = False
          .Italic = False
          .Underline = wdUnderlineNone
          .UnderlineColor = wdColorAutomatic
          .StrikeThrough = False
          .DoubleStrikeThrough = False
          .Outline = False
          .Emboss = False
          .Shadow = True
          .Hidden = False
          .SmallCaps = False
          .AllCaps = False
          .Color = wdColorRed
          .Engrave = False
          .Superscript = False
          .Subscript = False
          .Spacing = 0
          .Scaling = 100
          .Position = 0
          .Kerning = 0
          .Animation = wdAnimationNone
      End With
  End Sub
```

2. Make any necessary changes, save the changes and close the Visual Basic window.

The macro looks more complicated than it really is. However, you can use Visual Basic to create much more complex macros, using some very sophisticated programming principles. For more information on Visual Basic macros, see the on-line help.

Creating On-line Forms

What you will learn in this unit

A form is a document that has specified areas that are to be filled in so that you can collect and organise information. An on-line form can have text boxes to fill in, check boxes to select and clear, and drop-down boxes that contain lists of items from which to select answers. An on-line form needs to be created as a template so that it can be distributed to its target audience. You can also create a form that is printed and then filled in on paper.

The best way to create a form is by using tables. Tables enable layout, bordering and shading to be easily designed to give the form a professional appearance.

At the end of this unit you will be able to:

❑   Understand form fields.

❑   Design and create an on-line form.

Designing a form

Many forms, such as contracts, consist solely of text, with form fields inserted throughout the document so that users can provide specific information. Other forms are based on a grid, in which you can combine features such as tables to align text, borders to designate text areas to be filled in, and shading to emphasise headings and other special elements that make the form more attractive and easier to use. Examples of such forms would be invoices and purchase orders.

Form fields

There are three types of form field: text boxes, check boxes and list boxes.

❑   A text box is a field where the person filling in the form can enter text. A check box is where the box may be 'ticked' to indicate a choice.

❑   Check boxes may be grouped to form options where only one of a set of choices may be chosen.

❑   A list box is one that may be opened to reveal a list of choices.

You will be familiar with the use of all these types of form fields through using dialog boxes.

Forms toolbar

When creating a form, you will need to display the Forms toolbar. To do this, choose **View-Toolbars**, tick the **Forms** box and click on **OK**.

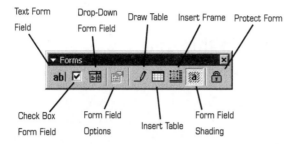

You may wish to drag the toolbar to a convenient location on the screen, possibly at the end of another toolbar such as the Borders toolbar. When you have finished your form, the Forms toolbar may simply be closed.

Creating a form

You can create forms that are filled in on-line or printed and then filled in on paper. On-line forms can be distributed and collected via electronic mail or other kinds of networks. You can add help messages to on-line forms to assist users.

Creating an on-line form

You *must* create and save an on-line form as a new *template* so that macros and AutoText entries are available to users who fill in the form. First sketch out a design for your form or base it on an existing form or template.

1. Create a template in one of these ways:

   ❑ Create a new template based on an existing document. Choose **File-Open** and then open the document you want.

   ❑ Base a new template on an existing template. Choose **File-New-More Word Templates**. Select a template that is similar to what you want or choose *Blank Document* (Normal template), choose the **Template** option and click on **OK**.

2. Choose **File-Save As**. In the **File Name** box, type a name for the new template.

3. In the **Save In** box, the *Templates* folder should be open. To add the template to a specific category of templates – e.g. *Chelmer Templates* – open the corresponding subfolder of the *Templates* folder.

4. In the **Save as type** box, select **Document Template** and click on **Save**.

5. Add any text and graphics that you want to appear in the forms that will be based on the template, and delete any items you don't want to appear.

6. Make any changes you want to the margin settings, page size and orientation, styles, and other formats. Save.

7. Add the form fields. For each form field you want to add, position the insertion point in the document at the point where you want users to insert information, and then click on the appropriate button in the form toolbar.

8. To set options for the form field, double-click the form field.

9. When you finish designing the form, click on the **Protect Form** button on the Forms toolbar, so that users can enter information only in the form fields.

10. Save and close the template.

If you create or modify AutoText entries and macros, make the items available only to documents based on the new template, not to all documents. Save changes to menu settings, shortcut keys, and toolbars in the new template, not the Normal template.

Form fields are shaded for easy identification. You can turn form field shading off or on by clicking on the **Form Field shading** button on the Forms toolbar.

Form fields

You can add as many fields as you like to each form.

Text form fields

A text form field is a field where users can enter text. You can specify a default entry so that the user does not have to type an entry except to change the response.

Options in a text field

Options in a text field can be specified in the Text Form Field Options dialog box which can be displayed by double-clicking on the form field or by clicking on the **Form Field shading** button in the Forms toolbar.

The **Type** list in the Text Form Field Options dialog box contains six field types you can use to achieve different results in a text form field.

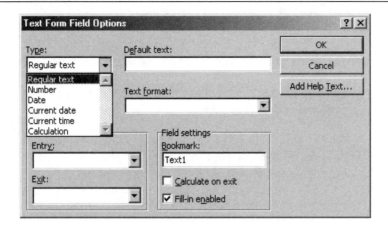

The types are as follows:

Option	Characteristics
Regular Text	Accepts text, numbers, symbols, or spaces.
Number	Requires a number.
Date	Requires a valid date.
Current Date/ Current Time	Displays current date or time. Users cannot fill in or change this field.
Calculation	Uses an = (Formula) field to calculate numbers, such as the VAT on a subtotal. Users cannot fill in or change this field.

Through the **Default text** and **Maximum length** boxes additional specifications can be given to the expected text response. Text may be formatted to be upper case, lower case, or first letter upper case using the settings in the **Text format** box. Macros can be attached to a text box to run either on the text box being activated (*Entry*) or on the text box being deactivated as another part of the form is selected (*Exit*).

Pressing the **Add Help Text** button will display the **Form Field Help Text** dialog box. Here you can type help messages which appear either in the status bar when the field is selected or when *F1* is pressed.

Check box fields

A check box field is where users can express a yes/no response in terms of a tick or a blank. Usually the tick indicates a 'yes' and the blank a 'no'. A check box is put next to a suitable item of text. If you use more than one check box in a form they are independent, so that the perrson filling the form can select any number of them.

Options in a check box field

Double-clicking on a check box field will display the Check Box Form Field Options dialog box. Through this dialog box you can alter the size of the check box, set its default value to not checked or checked, attach macros and add help text.

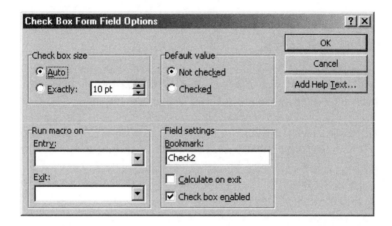

List box fields

A list box field, when activated, gives the user a drop-down list of choices which they can scroll through to select their response. The user is restricted to the choices that you supply in the drop-down list.

Options in a drop-down list box field

Through the Options dialog box, displayed by double-clicking on the field, the items in the drop-down list are created. Type the first item into the **Drop-down item** box and click on the **Add>>** button. Repeat this to add all the items to the list. To change the order of items in the list, use the two **Move** buttons. It is best to put those most likely to be chosen nearer the top. If you wish to delete an item, select it in the **Items** in drop-down list and click on **Remove**.

In common with the other field types, macros can be attached and help text added.

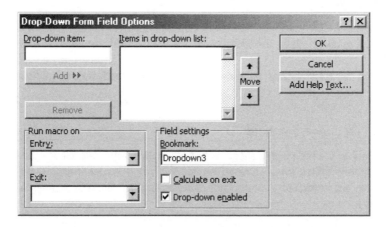

Retrieving the data

Forms are filled in by creating documents based on the form templates and saving these in the usual way. (You can add a toolbar button with a suitable macro attached to speed up the process of document creation.)

Data that is entered into an on-line form may either be printed or saved for exporting to a spreadsheet or database. To print the data from an on-line form:

1. Open the document saved from the form template and choose **Tools-Options** and select the **Print** tab.

2. Tick the **Print data only for forms** check box, click on **OK** and print the data. Word prints only the data entered in an on-line form, and no other part of the form.

If you based the design of the on-line form on a preprinted form, such as a company invoice or record sheet, and provided that the form fields appear in the same locations, you can insert the blank preprinted forms in a printer and use this procedure to fill in the preprinted forms.

Save the data from an on-line form for use in a spreadsheet or database as follows:

1. Open the document that was filled in as an on-line form. Choose **Tools-Options** and select the **Save** tab.

2. Tick the **Save data only for forms** check box and click on **OK**.

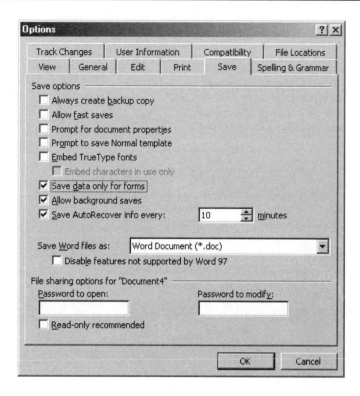

3. Choose **File-Save Copy As** and type a filename in the **File name** box.

4. In the **Save as type** box, select **Text Only**. Word saves the form field data in a comma-delimited text file, which can be imported into a spreadsheet or database for analysis.

Task 1: A simple customer details on-line form

This task creates a form template that invites a prospective house purchaser to give their details. Text fields are used to request name and address details, check box fields are used to request customer preferences, and a drop-down list box is used to find out why they have chosen to place their custom with Chelmer Estates.

Exact instructions are not given, as you should be familiar with formatting and creating tables. Create the form template as follows:

1. Choose **File-New-More Word Templates**, click to select the **Template** option and with *Blank Document* highlighted click on **OK**.

2. Choose **File-Save** and select **Document Template** in the **Save as type** box. Save in the *Chelmer Templates* folder as **Customer details form**. Click on **Save**.

CustomerDetails

*If you would like us to add your details
to our mailing list so that we can send
you up-to-date details of our
comprehensive list of properties, please
take five minutes to complete this form.*

Your name:				
Title: **Mr** ⬥	Initials: ▬	Lastname: ▬		25/09/2001
Your address:				
Street: ▬		Town: ▬		
County: ▬		Postcode: ▬		
Check this box if you are a first time buyer: ☐				
Type of property you are interested in:				
Leasehold ☐		Freehold ☐		
Detached ☐		Semi-detached ☐	Bungalow ☐	
Terrace ☐		Flat/apartment ☐		
Please indicate your preferred price range:				
£30,000-£50,000 ☐		£50,000-£70,000 ☐	£70,000-£100,000 ☐	
£100,000-£150,000 ☐		£150,000-£250,000 ☐	£250,000 and above ☐	

*Thank you for your co-operation. Please save the form by double-clicking **here***

3. Add a Chelmer Estates logo to the form. Make it a floating image with square text wrapping. Add the instructions at the top of the form.

4. Put the body of the text in a table.

5. Display the Forms toolbar. Add form fields as necessary. To add a form field, position the insertion point and then click on the appropriate button in the Forms toolbar. Set appropriate text formatting for the text box fields, e.g. *First capital* for names and *Uppercase* for initials and postcode. Use **Insert-Date and Time** to add the current date.

6. You may wish to experiment with adding help text: for example, in the *Freehold* and *Leasehold* check boxes to explain the meanings of these terms.

7. Finally, add a macro button field which, when double-clicked, would run the **File-Save** command. Use **Insert-Field**, choose the **Document Automation** category and select **Macro button**.

8. Click on **Options** and choose **FileSave**, click on **Add to Field** and add the word 'here' to act as the display text. Click on **OK** on each dialog box.

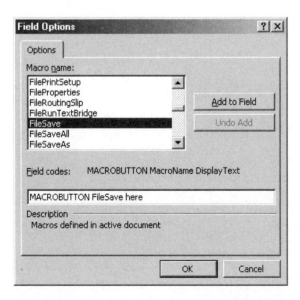

9. Include a reference in small type as the first line of the document so that this is used as the basis for the filename.

10. Click on the **Protect Form** button of the Forms toolbar and then save the completed template.

11. Test the template by using **File-New-More Word Templates** and selecting the *Customer details form* to give a blank form. Fill in the form and save as a normal document.

12. Open the completed form and save it as a comma-delimited text file.

13. Add a macro to create a new document based on the form template. Attach the macro to a toolbar button.

Group Working

What you will learn in this unit

In this era of network communication, and documents passing through a number of electronic versions, document creation is often a shared process. Within organisations, a manager may key some basic text through the keyboard and then e-mail that text as an attached document to a secretary, who may undertake corrections and formatting, and then return the text for comment; the manager may suggest final corrections. Alternatively, documents may be shared amongst a group; members of the group may have different levels of read and write access. Word's 'Comments' feature can be valuable in allowing people to mark up documents. Version control and security are, however, particularly necessary. It is important to be able to identify the latest version of a document, and to be confident that only those people who should have access to a document do so.

At the end of this unit you will be able to:

❑ Use comments and alterations in exchanging documents between multiple authors.

❑ Print document version information and statistics.

❑ Be able to use e-mail to send documents to others.

❑ Protect documents using passwords.

Although the features in this unit are most valuable for those who work in a networked environment, they can also be useful to those who work alone.

What you need

To complete this unit you will need:

❑ The document file *Pattison D V&S* created in Unit 3

Using comments

Electronic comments perform much the same function as comments on paper documents. The only additional feature supports multiple comments from several authors; since it is no longer possibly to recognise their handwriting, it is necessary that they be identified through their user name. Accordingly each annotation has an associated user name. Once comments have been inserted into a document they may be saved with the document. When the document is returned to its original author, the author can read the annotation by running the pointer over the text.

The locations of comments are marked with yellow highlighting and, when the pointer is passed over the text, the comments themselves are shown in a box.

To insert a comment, position the pointer immediately after the relevant word (before any space):

1. Choose **Insert-Comment**. Alternatively, display the Reviewing toolbar, using **View-Toolbars- Reviewing**, and click on the **Insert Comment** button.

2. In the **Comments from** box, check that your correct user name is identified. Type in your comment in the space in the lower half of the screen.

3. Click on **Close** and the annotation will be inserted in the text.

Instead of text comments, you can insert a sound file as an audio comment. After step 1 above, click on the **Insert Sound Object** button in the Comment toolbar and then you can either record a message directly (provided you have a soundcard and microphone) or you can attach an existing file. Note that this could significantly increase the size of your document.

Task 1: Inserting comments into text

1. Open the letter created in Unit 3 (saved as *Pattison D V&S*).

2. Display the Reviewing toolbar. Click on the **Insert Comment** button on the Comment toolbar.

3. Choose the correct user name and type in a comment.

4. Switching between the comment window and the document, move the insertion point, click on the **Insert Comment** button, and type in further comments in the Comment window.

5. Click on **Close**.

6. Check that your comments are as you planned by moving the insertion point over the text. Save the document.

The Reviewing (Comment) toolbar

The Comment toolbar offers a range of buttons.

The functions of most of these buttons are clear. These fall into two categories:

❑ Managing comments, including **Insert Comment**, **Edit Comment**, **Previous Comment**, **Next Comment** and **Delete Comment**.

❑ Managing alterations to the text, including **Track Changes** (when this button is clicked any changes are displayed in blue and can be identified as such), **Previous Change**, **Next Change**, **Accept Change** (causes the selected change to be integrated into the text) and **Reject Change** (deletes the change).

The toolbar also includes buttons to allow you to:

❑ Change the highlight colour.

❑ Create a Microsoft Outlook task.

❑ Save versions.

❑ Send to mail recipient.

Task 2: Deleting comments

Open the document that you were using in Task 1 and, by selecting each comment in turn, delete the comments.

Use the right-click shortcut menu and select **Delete Comment** in each case. Resave the document.

Tracking changes

The Reviewing toolbar allows you to track changes made to the document. After you have switched tracking on, any changes you make are highlighted. You can then inspect each of the changes in turn and decide whether or not to accept the alterations. (Another author might often perform this process after the version had been e-mailed to them by the person proposing the alterations.)

Task 3: Making alterations

To track the changes you make to a document:

1. Open the letter *Pattison D V&S*.

2. Click on the **Track Changes** button and make six alterations to the text of the letter used in Task 2.

Dear Mrs Pattison

Re: 34 Cedar Close, Chelmer, Cheshire

We write as promised to confirm our comments with regard to value and saleability of the above mentioned property.

We found the property to comprise a modern semi-detached dwelling, with extensive gardens to rear.

We regard valuation as lying reasonably in the region of £75,000£80,000 and would suggest an initial asking price of £78,000£83,000 subject to contract, as a test of market reaction.

We enclose our terms and conditions in accordance with the Estate Agents Act 1979, Section 18 as amended with effect from 29th July 1991. If there are any aspects of these terms that you wish to discuss please do not hesitate to get in touch. We trust you found our comments helpful and look forward to hearing from you.

Yours sincerely

H. D. Jones B.A., E.N.A.E.A
Director
Chelmer Estates

---

3. Review your alterations and accept or reject each in turn. View the alterations by clicking on the **Next Change** button; then use the **Accept Change** or **Reject Change** button.

4. Save the revised letter.

Version information

Saving a file with **File-Version** gives you the opportunity to specify details of the current version of the document. A dialog box is displayed, in which the previous version details are listed.

Click on **Save Now** and you will be able to add a version description. This includes the date and time that the version is saved and who it has been saved by, and allows you to insert any comments on the revised version.

This information will be added to the **File-Version** dialog box.

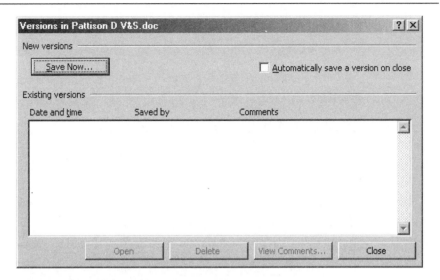

Task 4: Saving versions

Load the letter from the previous task and save it with **File-Version**. Make further changes and save a new version. Notice how the version information is built up each time you use this command.

Printing document information and statistics

You may wish to print a draft of a document with comments, or just print the comments alone. In addition, when documents are subject to several drafts, possibly with the intervention of a number of authors, it is important to be able to identify which version of the document is currently being viewed or printed. Document information and statistics are designed to assist you to differentiate between different documents and different versions of a document. You can print document information, such as document properties, comments, field codes, hidden text or drawing objects, either with or without the text of the document.

To print only the document information:

1. Choose **File-Print**.

2. In the **Print what** box, click on, for example, **Document Properties** or **Comments**.

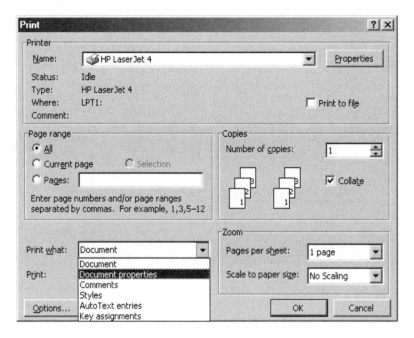

To print document information together with the document:

1. Choose **Tools-Options-Print**.

2. Select the option **Include with Document** and select the items to be included.

Once you have changed the **Tools-Option-Print** settings they stay changed for anything you print in future. So, until you change them back again, document information sheets will accompany every letter, memo or other document you print out.

You can display various statistics relating to a document by selecting **File-Properties** and clicking on the **Statistics** tab.

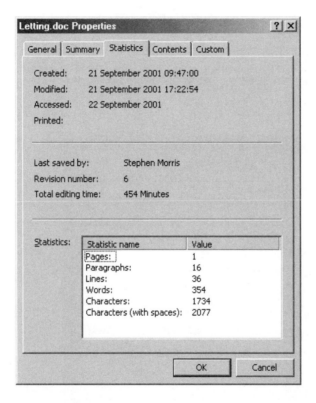

Task 5: Printing comments

1. Open the letter from the previous task and insert several comments in the text of the document.

2. Print the comments with the text of the document.

3. Now print the comments alone.

Whether you choose to print the whole document or the comments alone depends on the length of the document and the extent of the alterations. With the short one-page document that you have used above, it is easier to print the comments together with the document. In a long document with only a few comments, it is usually more effective and economical just to print the comments.

4. To complete this task, you may like to try to print document properties which will give information about the document, such as:

❏ Filename, Directory (folder), Template

❏ Title, Subject, Author

❏ Keywords, Comments

❏ Creation Date, Change number

❏ Last Saved On, Last Saved By, Last Printed On.

To edit properties such as Title, Subject, Author and Keywords use **File-Properties**.

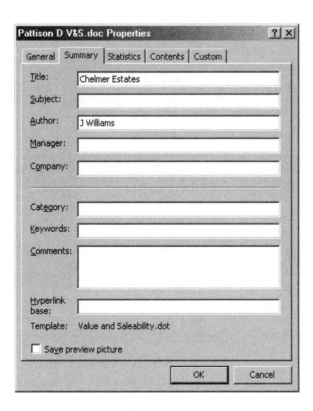

E-mailing documents as attached files

Word documents can be sent as files attached to an e-mail message, using a number of different e-mail systems. There are generally two different ways to do this, and depending on the compatibility of your e-mail system with the system of the recipient of your messages, you may find it necessary to experiment with different approaches. The two main methods are as follows:

1. In your e-mail package window, write a message, and then attach a file using the **Attach** option available in the e-mail package.

2. Using **File-Send To**, choose the option **Mail recipient** to send your document as an attached file. If you are using Outlook, an e-mail dialog box will appear with an icon for the document in the Message section. Complete and send the message as normal, adding your message text after the document icon.

    If you have not used the e-mail system from within Word, this procedure may take you into the Set up Wizard. Just follow the steps in this wizard to prepare for e-mailing.

The task below demonstrates how the **File-Send To** option can he used to send messages in Microsoft Outlook, the e-mail package within the Office suite.

While many of the recipients of your e-mail messages may work with Word, they will have a variety of different versions of Word, and others may work with other word-processing packages. It will help your recipient if you save your document in a file format that they can import into their word-processing package. If you cannot choose exactly the right format, rich text format (*.rtf*) files are often a good alternative.

Task 6: E-mailing attached documents

For this task, you need to be able to e-mail your document to someone else.

1. Open the letter that we have been using throughout this unit.

2. Using **File-Send To**, send your document as an attached file to someone else. Ask them to send it back to you (including the attachment).

3. Click on the icon for the attached document. This will open the document in Word.

    Sometimes such attached documents do not appear with full formatting. In order to display this, you may need to save the document as a Word, and then to open this new file.

Protecting documents

There are several ways in which you can restrict access to a document using a password. A password is case sensitive and can contain up to 15 characters. You can do any of the following:

❏ Prevent unauthorised users from opening the document by assigning a password to open the document.

❑ Prevent another user from modifying a document. Another user can read the document but they cannot save any changes without using a password. If the user opens the document without the password they can read the document and can only save the document by giving it a different filename.

❑ Recommend that others open the document as a read-only file. If they agree to open the document as a read-only file and do change it, the document can only be saved by giving it a different filename. If they don't agree to open the document as a read-only file, the document opens as a normal read-write file and changes can be saved with the document's original filename.

❑ Assign a password when you route a document for review, which prevents any changes, except by authorised users, for comments or tracked changes. This can be set using **Tools-Protect Document**.

 If you assign password protection to a document and then forget the password, you can't open the document, remove protection from it, or recover data from it. It's a good idea to keep a list of your passwords and their corresponding document names in a safe place.

To protect a document:

1. Open the document you wish to protect. Choose **File-Save As** and click on the **Tools** button. Select **General Options** from the menu.

2. To protect a document from being *opened* by an unauthorised user enter the password into the **Password to open** box.

3. To protect a document from being *modified* by an unauthorised user enter the password into the **Password to modify** box.

4. To give the user the choice of opening the document as read only or not, check the **Read-only recommended** box.

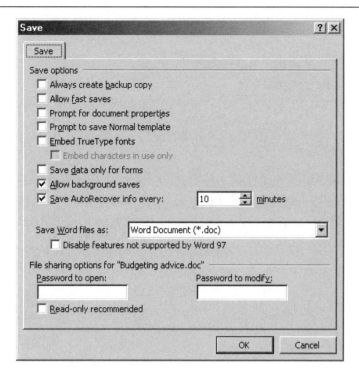

Task 6: E-mailing attached documents

This task saves a document with a password.

1. Open the letter *Pattison D V&S.*

2. Choose **File-Save As**. Click on the **Tools** button. Select **General Options** from the menu.

3. Type a password in the **Password to open** box. The characters you type appear as asterisks. Press *Enter*. Make sure you choose a password you can remember and check that *Caps Lock* is not switched on.

4. You are asked to retype the password. Type it again and press *Enter*.

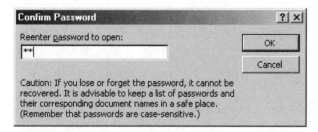

5. Click on **Save**. Close the document.

6. Open the letter again. You are asked to enter the password.

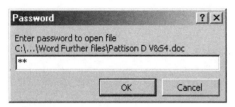

7. Type the password and press *Enter*. Providing you have remembered the password correctly, the document will open.

Using Organisation Charts

What you will learn in this unit

We have already met a number of 'objects' that might be embedded in a Word document such as a Word picture or a Word chart. Both these objects have an associated application which allow you to create and edit the object. Similarly Equation Editor (described in *Word 2000 Basic Skills*) creates an equation object within a document. Organization Chart is a further example of objects that can be created and embedded in a Word document and later edited.

Organization Chart is a special graphics tool which supports the creation of organisational charts. This tool is also available to the other applications within Office.

By the end of this unit you will be able to:

❑ Use Organization Chart to create structure charts.

❑ Extend and edit organisation charts.

Organisational charts

An organisational chart is one that is used to show the structure of an organisation. These structures are hierarchical with, say, a managing director at the top level and each succeeding level representing a lower level of management. As there are generally more managers at the lower levels, this chart takes on a 'root-like' (upside-down tree) structure. An example of a simple structure is shown below.

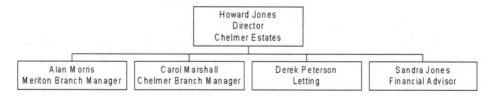

Chelmer Estates Management Structure

Starting Microsoft Organization Chart

To enable you to add professional organisational charts to your documents, Microsoft Office supplies an application called MS Organization Chart 2.0. This application is used to create a chart, which is embedded into a document when complete. An embedded organisational chart may be revisited later if editing is required.

To start Microsoft Organization Chart, choose **Insert-Object** and select **MS Organization Chart 2.0**.

The Organization Chart application starts with a default chart displayed. Use the **View** menu to alter the size of the default chart to suit.

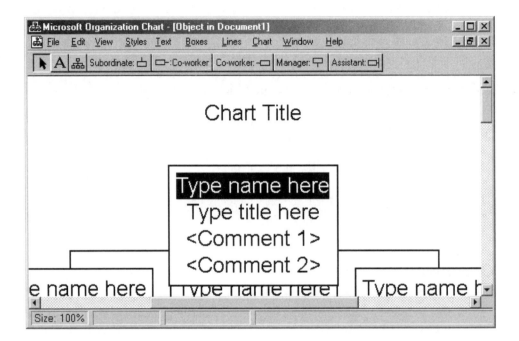

 When working with the chart window it is useful to click on its Maximize button to prevent accidental clicking on the document window behind.

Selecting and entering information into chart boxes

Before any editing or reformatting of chart boxes can be performed, the boxes must be selected. When the default chart loads, the top level box is selected and appears highlighted.

To	Do this
Select one box	Click on the box.
Select a set of boxes	Drag a selection rectangle around the boxes.
Select the whole chart	Choose **Edit-Select All**.
Select one level or one branch of the chart	Choose **Edit-Select** and **All Managers**, **Branch** or **Lowest Level**.

With a chart box selected, text may be entered. When the box is clicked a larger text box appears with the following placeholders:

Type name here
Type title here
<Comment 1>
<Comment 2>

To alter the placeholder text, highlight it by clicking and dragging and then type in the required text. The comment lines are optional; if no text is added to them they do not appear on the chart. When the text is added click on a blank part of the screen to add the box into the chart.

Embedding the organisation chart into the document

When the organisation chart is complete it can be embedded into the document and then saved. As you need to embed the chart before saving it may be useful to do this before the chart is complete, particularly for a complex chart. An embedded chart can easily be re-opened for editing by double-clicking on it.

To embed a chart into a document use **File-Exit and Return to *filename***. Answer **Yes** to the 'Update object in file' dialog query.

Task 1: Creating a simple organisation chart

This task creates the chart illustrated above.

1 . Start a new document. Choose **Insert-Object** and select **MS Organization Chart 2.0**. Click on **OK**. If you wish to add an organisation chart to an existing document, position the insertion point at the required place and follow the steps above. The chart can be re-positioned within the document later.

2. Click on the Maximize button of the Organization Chart window.

3. Select the top level box by clicking on it.

4. Double-click on the selected top level box to display the text box. Select the first three text placeholders in turn and replace them with:

Howard Jones
Director
Chelmer Estates

5. Now click on a blank part of the screen.

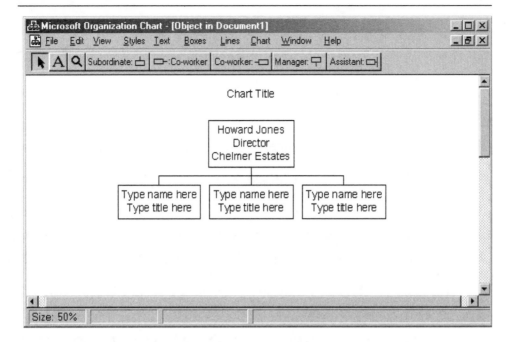

6. Repeat the process for the other lower level boxes adding the following people to the chart: *Alan Morris, Meriton Branch Manager; Carol Marshall, Chelmer Branch Manager;* and *Derek Peterson, Letting. Sandra Jones* will be added in the next task.

7. In the same way, edit the **Chart Title** (select then type) to read: *Chelmer Estates Management Structure.*

8. Choose **File-Exit and Return to document** and click on **Yes** to update the chart in the document. Save the document as *Chelmer Estates Management Structure.*

Adding and deleting chart boxes

The default organisational chart is unlikely to be the structure that you require and you will wish to modify it by adding and removing boxes and levels. The tasks below concentrate on simple structure charts and use the buttons on the Organization toolbar to create such charts. These buttons are summarised in the following table:

Button	Function
Subordinate:	Click on this button and then click on the chart box for which you wish to create a lower level.
:Co-worker Co-worker:	Click one or other of these buttons to add an extra box to the right or left of the selected chart box.

Button	Function
Manager: ⊓	Click on this button and then click on the chart box above which you wish to create a higher level. Note: the box you click on is demoted.
Assistant: ⊐⊣	Click on this button and then on the box to which you wish to add an assistant box.

Deleting boxes

To delete a structure chart box, select the box and delete it by pressing the *Delete* key. Note that if a box is deleted which has subordinate levels, these are not deleted; they move up one level.

To cater for more variety in a chart, different group styles may be chosen from the **Styles** menu. An example of a vertical group style can be seen in the chart illustrated in Task 4.

Task 2: Adding a co-worker

Open the document *Chelmer Estates Management Structure*.

1. Double-click on the organisation chart to run MS Organization Chart 2.0.

2. Click on the **Right Co-worker** button and then click on the right-hand box of the second level to create an extra box at that level.

3. Add the following text to this box:

> Sandra Jones
> Financial Advisor

4. Return to the document and save it.

Task 3: Adding co-managers to a chart

The aim of this task is to create the structure shown below. This chart has a co-manager level.

1. Start a new document and choose **Insert-Object**, select **MS Organization Chart 2.0** and click on **OK**.

2. Delete two of the lower-level boxes by selecting them and pressing the *Delete* key. Note two or more boxes may be selected at once by holding down the *Shift* key during the selection process.

3. Click on the one remaining subordinate box and choose **Co-manager** from the **Styles** menu.

Meriton Branch Organisation Structure

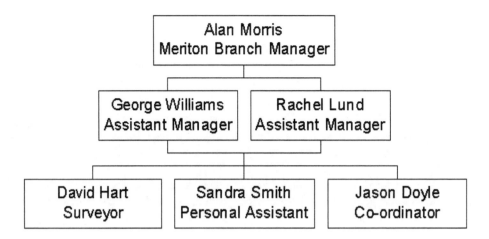

4. Click on the **Subordinate** button and click on the top-level box, thereby creating two co-managers.

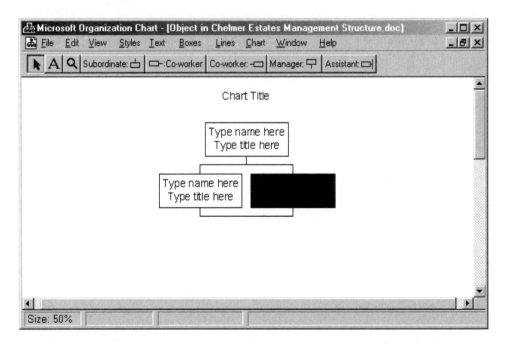

5. Click on the **Subordinate** button and add a subordinate to the co-managers by clicking on one of them. Repeat to add another two subordinates.

6. Add the text, names and positions as illustrated. Embed the chart in the document and save as *Organisation chart examples*.

Task 4: Adding groups of co-workers

In this task a second chart will be added to the document *Organisation chart examples*. This chart illustrates a different type of organisation.

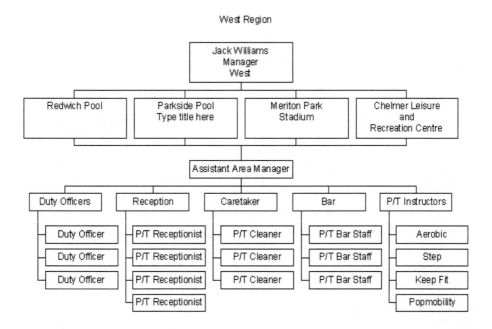

1. Open the document *Organisation chart examples*, make a blank line beneath the last chart and using **Insert-Object** add a second chart.

2. To select the boxes at level 2 choose **Edit-Select levels** and choose **2 through 2**.

3. Open the **Styles** menu and select **Co-manager**. Choose a **Left Co-worker** and click on the left-hand co-manager to create four co-managers.

4. Click on the **Subordinate** button and click on one of the co-managers. Click on the **Subordinate** button again and add a subordinate of the last subordinate. Add four additional co-workers (as illustrated below).

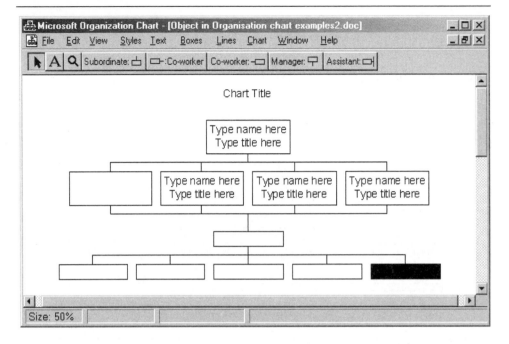

5. Click on the **Subordinate** button and click on the left-hand box at the lowest level. Choose **Styles** and click on the top middle button (vertical group). Click on **Left Co-worker** and add a co-worker to this box. Repeat to add the third co-worker.

6. Add the other lowest-level vertical groups in the same way as described above.

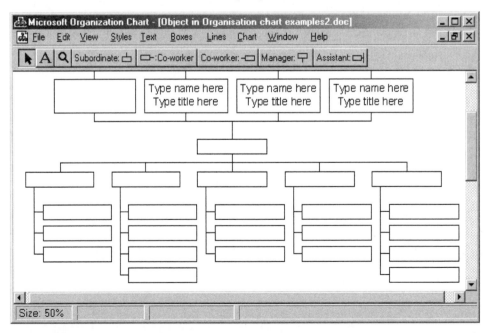

7. Add the text to the boxes, return to the document and save.

Editing an organisational chart

Text in the boxes in an organisational chart can be edited and its font, alignment and colour can be altered using the **Text** menu. The colour, line style and shadow effects of the boxes can be changed using the **Boxes** menu. The background colour of the whole chart can be set using the **Chart** menu.

Task 5: Editing colours, line styles and shadows

1. Open the document *Chelmer Estates Management Structure*. Double-click on the chart to edit it. Select the top level box. Using **Text-Font**, alter the font of the text. As the whole box is selected all the text in the box will reflect the change you make. Try selecting a portion of the text within the box and altering its font. You will find that only the selected text is changed.

2. Investigate changing the colour of the text using **Text-Color**.

3. Select all the boxes using **Edit-Select Levels** and change the colour of the box background using **Boxes-Color**. If you wish to experiment then select different levels and apply different colours to the boxes. Remember, however, that for a serious chart too many colours will look gaudy so colours should be chosen with care. If in doubt, choose fewer rather than more colours.

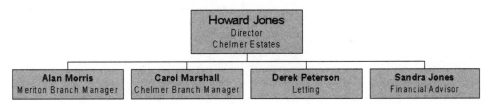

Chelmer Estates Management Structure

4. Select boxes and levels and investigate the options in the **Boxes** menu. Again take care when choosing these for a serious chart; err on the side of fewer effects to avoid making your chart look too busy.

5. Finally, through **Chart-Background Color** you may choose the background for the whole chart. When choosing this and other colours in the chart, take into account any other colours you have used your document.

6. Return to the document and save. Experiment with changing text, colour and line style in the other two charts created in this unit.

Producing HTML Documents

What you will learn in this unit

This unit is the first of several that will introduce you to the process of creating documents, known as HyperText Markup Language (HTML) documents, for publication on the World Wide Web. Such documents may be used in both Internet and Intranet (within one organisation) applications.

Producing Web or HTML documents using Word's Web authoring tools is very much like producing a normal document. An HTML document does not support the range of word processing features that normal documents do, as the aim is to keep them simple for transmission over the Internet.

This unit concentrates on basic document production and posting a document on to a World Wide Web (WWW) server. By the end of this unit you will be able to:

❑ Create a basic HTML document.

❑ Convert an existing Word document to an HTML document.

❑ Create a suitable directory structure for storage of HTML documents.

Web authoring tools are available with Word. If they are not available then install them from the Office CD. The Web authoring tools allow you to create HTML documents without having to learn HTML itself. HTML is a set of codes that are embedded in a plain text file, in order to tell an Internet browser how to display them on screen. A browser is a software application that retrieves and displays files on the Internet; familiarity with browser software is assumed in this and the units that follow.

Many HTML codes are concerned with the formatting of text. By selecting styles provided by the Web authoring tools these codes are automatically embedded in the document. In this unit we will concern ourselves with the production of small one page (or one screen) documents. In the next unit the concept of pages and their use in a Web-publishing context will be considered.

What you need

To complete this unit you will need:

❑ The document file *Budgeting advice* as amended in Unit 4

The Web Wizard

The quickest way to create a web page is to make use of the Web Wizard. However, in most applications it will be necessary to design unique Web pages, either by designing a page from the beginning or by formatting a Web page that has been created through the use of the Web Wizard. In order to demonstrate more fully the formatting of Web pages, the next few sections create a Web page without the support of the wizard. We recommend that you return to the use of the wizard after you have completed the tasks in this and the following units.

To use the wizard choose **File-New-More Word Templates**, select the **Web Pages** tab and double-click on the *Web Page Wizard*. This will open a new HTML document and display a list of Web Page Layouts for you to choose from. Once you have chosen the type of layout, you can select a style, which will set fonts and background. You can then edit the document by replacing the example text with your own.

Task 1: Creating and saving a new HTML document using the Web Wizard

This task generates a set of Web pages using the Web Wizard.

1. Choose **File-New-More Word Templates**, select the **Web Pages** tab and double-click on the *Web Page Wizard*.

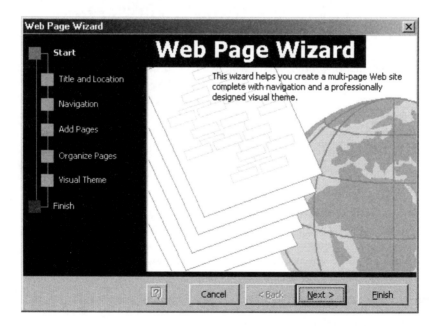

2. Click on **Next**. Enter *Selling your home* as the **Web site title**. If necessary, change the location for the files. (The wizard suggests a new folder name based on the site title you have entered.)

3.   Click on **Next**. Choose **Separate page** for the type of navigation.

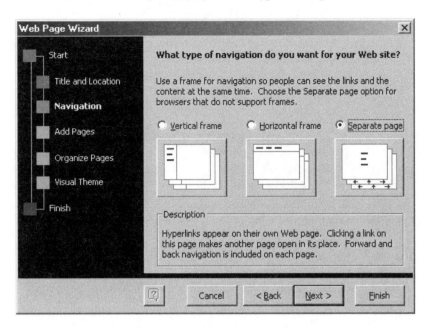

4.   Click on **Next** three times to get to the Visual Theme step. Click on **Browse Themes** and choose the *Industrial* theme. Click on **OK**.

5. Click on **Next** and **Finish**. The wizard creates all the necessary files and folders for you and displays the first Web page.

6. Replace the text with that illustrated below and save. Note that the links point to the other pages created by the wizard. Setting up links is described in Unit 18.

Selling your home?

At Chelrner Estates we offer you a service designed to meet your individual needs. We aim to achieve a successful sale of your property by providing a professional marketing strategy.

At Chelmer Estates we offer:

- Free valuation.
- A friendly team of experts.
- A complete property service.

Click on one of the agencies below for more information about your local branch.

Chelmer
Meriton
Branford

Creating a new HTML document

As an alternative to the Web Wizard, you can create an HTML document from scratch. Choose **File-New-More Word Templates** and choose a template from the **Web Pages** tab. When you choose a Web page a new document will open that has an HTML formatting toolbar.

Most buttons are the same as those in the Word document formatting toolbar but there are variations in the way some of the buttons and commands work.

Task 2: Creating and saving a new HTML document

This task creates a Web page with the styles *Normal, Heading 1* and *Heading 2*. Although Word offers the usual heading styles, many browsers use standard normal and heading styles so the resulting display of the text may differ from browser to browser.

The task creates the HTML document below.

Chelmer Estates Property Pages

8 Maple Mews, Maple Road, Meriton, Staffs

Asking Price £45,950

Reasonably priced two bedroomed apartment

Located within a purpose built two-storey block, this first floor flat provides an ideal opportunity to acquire a reasonably spacious flat within a competitive price range. Approached via a communal hallway leading to only four flats, the private accommodation is arranged around a central hallway with generous lounge, kitchen, two bedrooms and bathroom. **Gas fired central beating is installed.**

Location

From our Meriton office proceed along Chelmer Road turning right into Hornchurch Road. Continue along Rornchurch Road to the traffic lights, turn left into Blacksmith Lane and Maple Road is the third turning on the right. The property can be found on the right hand side.

Viewing by appointment only.

1. Choose **File-New-More Word Templates** and choose *Simple Layout* from the **Web Pages** tab. Click on **OK**.

2. Replace the first line with *Chelmer Estates Property Pages*. Delete the rest of the sample text.

3. On the next line select the style *Heading 2* and type in the property address. Use style *Heading 3* for the asking price and *Heading 4* for the next heading. Use the *Normal* style for the text paragraphs and *Heading 4* for the other heading. Make text bold in the same way as for Word documents.

4. Choose **File-Save**. Notice that *Web Pages (*.htm; *.html)* should be in the **Save as type** list box. (If necessary open the list box and select the file type *.htm*.)

5. Type the name of the document, *8 Maple Mews*, and click on **Save**. The file is saved with an htm extension.

   The codes given for the style name are the codes that are embedded in the document to tell the browser to display the text in a particular style. If you wish to see the codes, you can view the source code using **View-HTML Source**. (Save the document before you do this and use **View-Exit HTML Source** to return to the document.) However, if you wish to decipher them then you will need to refer to a book on HTML authoring. It is not necessary to learn these codes or 'tags' as the Web authoring tools can create the effects you require and more quickly.

Opening an existing HTML document

Closing and opening existing HTML documents is accomplished in exactly the same way as for Word documents. If you are not currently using the Web authoring tools you can open an HTML document using **File-Open** and selecting *Web Pages (*.htm; *.html)* from the **Files of type** list box. Select the file and click on **Open**. The document will open with the HTML formatting toolbar instead of the Word document formatting toolbar.

You may work with Word documents and HTML documents open at the same time and use the **Window** menu to switch between them; the appropriate formatting toolbar will be displayed for the active document.

Previewing a document using your browser

The **File-Web Page Preview** command allows you to view your document with Internet Explorer, the Microsoft browser, or any other browser installed on your computer. If the browser is not running then selecting this option will start the browser and display your document. If you have not saved your document you will be prompted to do so before the document is displayed. It is useful to preview your document from time to time as you might try to apply formatting which is ignored by the browser. As the level of sophistication of browsers increases then the formatting that they can display will probably also become more sophisticated. However, it is worth remembering that your target audience may be using a variety of browsers.

Close the browser when you have finished previewing.

Text formatting

As for Word documents, bold, italic and underlining may be applied to HTML documents. Text alignment – either left or centre – can be set using the alignment buttons.

To change the font (typeface), colour and size of any selected text, use the **Format-Font** command to display the Font dialog box. Use the drop-down list boxes to select the combination of formatting you require and click on **OK**.

Horizontal line

Lines provide a neat way of dividing up your Web page. A standard horizontal line or 'rule' can be added by selecting **Format-Borders and Shading** and then clicking on the **Horizontal Line** button. You can choose the line style. Click on **OK** to add the line.

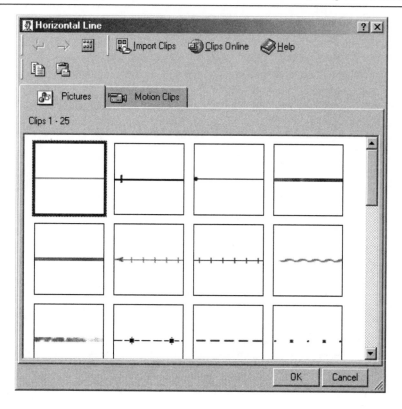

Task 3: Formatting and fonts

1. Open the document *8 Maple Mews* created in the last task. Position the insertion point at the end of the first heading. Select **Format-Borders and Shading** and click on the **Horizontal Line** button. Click on a suitable line and then on **OK**. Close the Borders and Shading dialog box. This should add a horizontal rule under this heading.

2. Select the last line and change the text to bold, italic. Click in the main heading and centre it by clicking on the **Center** button on the formatting toolbar. Save and preview in the browser.

Giving your document a title

Every HTML document (page) that you create should have a title. If you do not specify one, Word will use the filename. The title is the text that appears on the title bar of the browser window and would be used as a bookmark if anyone bookmarked your page when it is published on the Web.

If you wish to alter your document title, choose **File-Properties**, key the title into the **Title** box in the dialog box and click on **OK**.

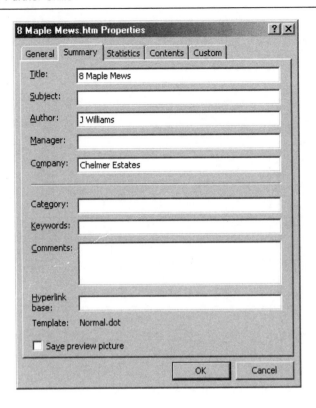

Converting an existing document to HTML format

Any document that you can open using Word can be converted to an HTML document. The Internet Assistant will, as far as possible, convert existing styles in your document to their HTML equivalent. Before converting a document it may be useful to review the styles used in it, perhaps using AutoFormat, although once converted you can easily re-assign styles to produce the required effect.

You may convert an existing document to HTML as follows:

1. Choose **File-Open**. Select the drive and directory where the document is stored. Select the file and click on **Open**.

2. Choose **File-Save As HTML**.

3. Choose the folder and either accept Word's choice of filename or type the name of your file and then click on **Save**.

Not all Word elements are preserved when a document is converted to HTML.

Task 4: Converting to HTML

In this task the document *Budgeting Advice* (as used in Unit 4) will be converted into an HTML document.

1. Open the file *Budgeting Advice* (Unit 4 version) and use **File-Save As** with the **Web Pages** type. The file is now named *Budgeting Advice.htm*. Change the title to *Budgeting Advice*.

2. Go through the document, apply some heading styles (*Heading 1* and *Heading 2* should be enough) and add some horizontal rules. Note that if the original document uses borders these will be converted to horizontal rules. Save and preview in the browser.

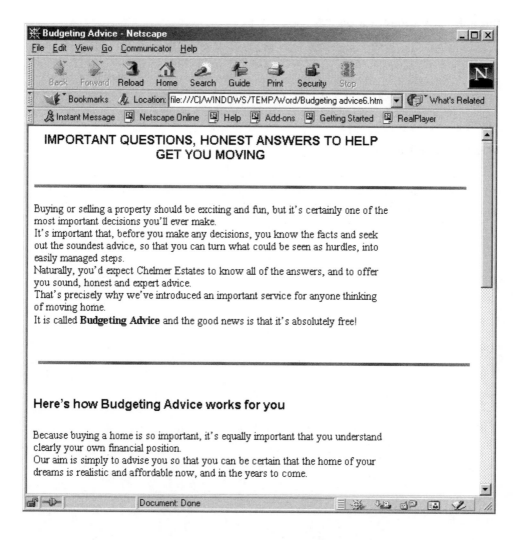

3. Review the document and make any further changes you require, for example colour and font. Save and preview it using your browser. Note that if the document

is already open in your browser you can use the browser's **Refresh** button to update to your current saved version.

Storing HTML documents

It is unlikely that you will store your entire Web publication in one htm file. In particular, if you wish to use graphics or other multi-media objects then these will be stored as separate files. It is easiest, particularly if you are new to Web publishing, to store all the files together in the same directory. In Unit 18 you will see how to create links between the files. If you keep files together in the same directory, then when you move them onto your service provider's Web server, the links between them will work as they did on your local directory.

Publishing a document on the Web

When you have completed your pages and tested them they will need to be uploaded to your service provider's computer. It is likely that you will be allocated one directory on that computer. You will need software for transferring files and this is available on the Web. The actual software you use may depend on your service provider but it is generally straightforward to use.

Viewing the HTML source

It is perfectly possible to create acceptable HTML documents using the Web authoring tools, but if you want to embellish the document then you can do so by editing the HTML source directly. In order to do this you will need to know more about mark-up tags, definitions of which are given in Word's on-line help.

Creating Linked HTML Pages

What you will learn in this unit

A document published on paper is usually read sequentially. Readers may often skip sections, however, or refer back to previous sections in the document that they are reading. Each Web document (page) is a file that is in electronic format, so, to give the viewer the ability to view your publication non-sequentially, you must provide links within and between pages.

If your page is large, you will want to provide the viewer with the ability to 'jump' to different headings within the page. Your viewer will also find it useful if you provide links back to the top of your document, so that they can 'jump' to another heading.

By the end of this unit you will be able to:

❏   Create links within a document.

❏   Create links to local files within your directory.

❏   Create links to other files on the Web.

What you need

To complete this unit you will need:

❏   The HTML document file *Budgeting advice.htm* created in Unit 17

Understanding links

A link is composed of two elements:

1.   A *destination* which may be:

❏   A place within the same document

❏   A local file (commonly image files, which are considered in the next unit)

❏   A file somewhere else on the Web

2.   A *tag* giving the name of the place to link to, which when activated invokes a 'jumping' action to that place. This is inserted into your document using the **Insert-Hyperlink** command. The link will appear as 'hot' text (graphics can also be used) which when clicked on will activate the 'jump'. 'Hot' text is usu-

ally a different colour from the normal text. In addition, the mouse pointer will change shape to a pointing finger when positioned over link text or graphics. If, when a link has been visited, your viewer returns to the previously displayed page, the linking text may be displayed in a different colour indicating that the link has been visited.

Creating links within the same document

To create links, you must provide destinations in your document for the 'jumps'. This is done by creating an 'anchor' in the text, using a bookmark. You may create several bookmarks within the document, usually at the beginning, the end and at each heading. When you add an anchor bookmark to an HTML document an anchor name tag is inserted into the source in the form:

<A NAME = "Contents"> Contents </A>

where <A NAME> is the anchor tag, "Contents" is the bookmark name and the one you will specify in your linking tag, and Contents is the text in the document to which the bookmark is attached.

Add a bookmark to your document as follows:

1. Position your insertion point at the beginning of the text (such as a heading) that you want to bookmark. Choose **Insert-Bookmark** and key in a name for your bookmark. Choose one that you will recognise when you later create links to it from other places in your document.

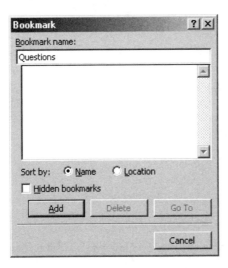

2. Click on **Add**. Repeat this process to add all the anchor bookmarks required in your document. Save your document and, if you wish, inspect the source to note the use of the tags.

Using the **Insert-Bookmark** command, bookmarks may be deleted or renamed (as described in Unit 5). As a document is revised you may wish to move a bookmark by deleting and re-creating it elsewhere. If you delete a bookmark altogether, or rename one, check that you also remove or edit link tags that refer to that bookmark.

The second stage is to add links to the document. When you add a link to an HTML document a Hypertext reference (HREF) tag is inserted into the source which, for a bookmark, is of the form:

    <A HREF="#Letting">Letting</A>

where *"#Letting"* is the anchor bookmark name and *Letting* is the link text that appears in the document.

Create links to bookmarks as follows:

1. Select the text that is to form the hyperlink. Choose **Insert-Hyperlink**.

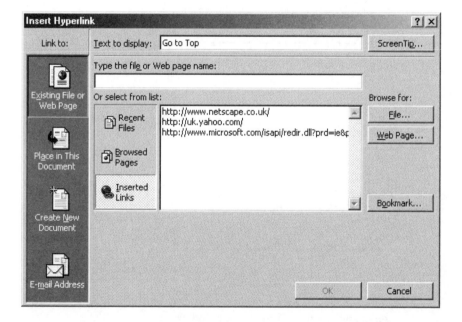

2. Click on the **Browse** button next to the **Named location in file** text box and select the bookmark you wish the link to refer to (and jump to if activated). Click on **OK**. The link text will appear underlined in a different colour (the default is blue).

3. Repeat this procedure to add all the links to the document and then save the document.

4. You may test your links by switching to Web Layout view (or selecting **File-Web Page Preview**) and clicking on the links.

Task 1: Creating links within a document

In this task, internal links will be created in the HTML document *Budgeting advice.htm* created in Unit 17.

1. Open *Budgeting advice.htm*.

2. Position your insertion point at the beginning of the first sub-heading. Choose **Insert-Bookmark** and key in the name *How_it_works* for the bookmark. As you cannot use a space in a bookmark name, an underscore makes a good substitute. Click on **Add**. Add bookmarks for the other sub-headings.

3. Position your insertion point at the beginning of the document. Choose **Insert-Bookmark**, key in *Top* for the bookmark and click on **Add**. Save.

4. Make a new line below the main heading and key in *How Budgeting Advice works* and select it. Choose **Insert-Hyperlink**.

5. Click on the **Bookmark** button and select the bookmark *How_it_works*. Click on **OK** twice.

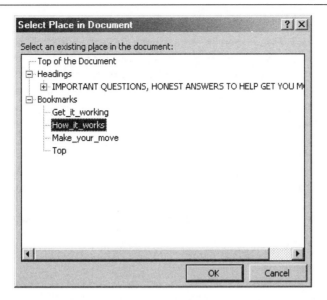

6. Add hyperlinks for the other sub-headings.

7. Make a new line at the end of the document and key in the text **Back to Top**. Select the word *Top*. Choose **Insert-Hyperlink**.

8. Click on the **Bookmark** button and select the bookmark *Top*. Click on **OK** twice. Save the document.

9. In Web Page Preview test out your links.

IMPORTANT QUESTIONS, HONEST ANSWERS TO HELP GET YOU MOVING

How Budgeting Advice works   Get Budgeting Advice working for you
Make your next move

Buying or selling a property should be exciting and fun, but it's certainly one of the most important decisions you'll ever make.

It's important that, before you make any decisions, you know the facts and seek out the soundest advice, so that you can turn what could be seen as hurdles, into easily managed steps.

Naturally, you'd expect Chelmer Estates to know all of the answers, and to offer you sound, honest and expert advice.

That's precisely why we've introduced an important service for anyone thinking of moving home.

It is called **Budgeting Advice** and the good news is that it's absolutely free!

Creating links to local files

Keeping all your HTML and graphics files in the same directory (folder) is the simplest approach in terms of creating links between them. However, if you have several graphics files you may wish to make a subdirectory (folder) to keep them in. As long as you keep the directory structure the same when you post your files on the Web you should not have any problems. If you view the HTML source code you will see that links to local files are achieved by tags of the form:

<A HREF="Guide.htm">Guidelines for publishing Web documents</A>

for a file in the same directory (folder) and:

<A HREF="Web/Guide.htm">Guidelines for publishing Web documents</A>

for a file in a subdirectory (folder) called *Web*. Note that directory (folder) separators are forward slashes.

The procedure for inserting a hyperlink to a local file is practically the same as that for a link within a document.

1. Select the text that is to form the hyperlink. Choose **Insert-Hyperlink**.

2. Click on the **File** button, select the directory (folder) in which the file is stored and select the file you wish the link to refer to (and open if activated). Click on **Open**. Click on **OK**. This will create a *relative* link.

3. Repeat this procedure to add to the document all links to local files and then save the document.

4. You may test your links by switching to Web Layout view and clicking on a link which will open the local file. Alternatively you can test them out using your browser (select **File-Web Page Preview**).

You can use this procedure to add links to normal word documents so that you can work with them in the same way as you would read HTML documents.

Task 2: Creating links with local documents

1. Create a home page for Chelmer Estates that looks similar to the example below. Save as *homepage.htm*.

2. Select the *Budgeting Advice* heading and choose **Insert-Hyperlink**.

3. Click on the **File** button and select the directory (folder) in which you saved the file *Budgeting advice.htm* (created in the last unit). Click on this file and then on **Open**. Note that it is best to keep all related files in the same directory. Click on **OK** and the link will be created. Save and test the link.

Chelmer Estates

Welcome to Chelmer Estates, with offices in Chelmer, Meriton, Branford and a new one opening soon in Oxley, we cover Cheshire, Staffordshire and Derbyshire. We are a long established (1965) firm and pride ourselves in our friendly efficient service. Don't delay in finding your new home, register with us now!

Property Pages

Budgeting Advice

A Guide to Selling your Home

A Guide to Letting your Home

Planning a Successful Move

Register on our Mailing list

4. Now create a link in the *Budgeting advice* file which will return the viewer to the home page. Save this file and test this link.

Creating links to files on the Web

You may wish to include links in your page to other sites on the Web. To do this you will need to enter the URL (Uniform Resource Locator) in the **File or Web page name** text box of the Hyperlink dialog box.

These are files over which you have no control so, before you create hyperlinks, it's a good idea, if possible, to check with the authors of the pages to which you are linking. They might have good reasons for you not to link to their pages: they may, for example, be planning to move or delete the page.

Even if you don't let the author of a page know that you are linking to his or her site, you should check all the links on your pages periodically. The Web is constantly in flux, and readers commonly experience the frustration of following links that lead to dead ends because the files have moved or been deleted. It is good Web publishing practice to try to save your viewers this frustration.

Before you begin this procedure, save the file in which you are creating the hyperlink.

To create links to Web files:

1. Select the text which is to form the hyperlink. Choose **Insert-Hyperlink**.

2. In the **File or Web page name** box, type the URL of the file you have chosen as the destination of your hyperlink. This must be absolutely precise, including upper and lower case and punctuation. Alternatively, use the **File** button to search for the page you wish to link to. Click on **OK**.

3. Repeat this procedure to add all links to Web files to the document and save the document. Test out the links and do not forget to check regularly that they still work.

Task 3: Creating links with Web documents

Browse the Web to find several sites that interest you, preferably on the same theme. Switch to Word and create a simple HTML document into which links to these sites can be added. Select the text you wish to make a hyperlink and choose **Insert-Hyperlink**. Using the **File** button, locate the page that interests you and click on **OK**. Save this document as *My interests* and test it.

Designing HTML Documents

What you will learn in this unit

Despite the fairly basic text-handling capabilities associated with HTML documents, they do cater for the use of lists, tables and graphics. Using these features, and particularly with good use of colour, the very attractive documents that are seen on many Web sites can be produced. If you are inexperienced at document design the best way to start is to look at other peoples' documents and model your designs on the ones that you find attractive. Do not be too ambitious initially; start with some relatively simple designs and build on these.

By introducing lists, tables, graphics and multimedia this unit aims to give you a basis from which you can begin to experiment with design features. At the end of this unit you will be able to:

❏   Add numbered and nested lists to an HTML page.

❏   Add tables to an HTML page.

❏   Insert an image into an HTML page.

❏   Add sound and video clips.

What you need

To complete this unit you will need:

❏   The document file *Code of Practice* created in Unit 6

❏   The document file *Price List* created in Unit 10

❏   The HTML file *homepage.htm* created in Unit 18

Lists

There are three types of list that you may want to include in an HTML document:

❏   Bulleted lists

❏   Numbered (or lettered) lists

❏   Lists of terms and definitions

Adding a bulleted or numbered list is simple, using the buttons on the toolbar as you would for a normal word document and switching off the numbering (or bulleting) when finished. Alternatively, you can key in the text for the list, select it and use the **Format-Bullets and Numbering** command.

If you want to use Roman numerals or letters for a 'numbered' list you can select these through the **Numbered** tab of the Bullets and Numbering dialog box. Bullets may be changed in similar way, but if you choose a graphic for a bullet then note that the source code for the list is different from that for a standard bulleted list.

The underlying source code for a numbered or standard bulleted list is of the form shown in the following table.

Standard Bulleted List	Numbered List
<UL>	<OL>
<LI>First item	<LI>First item
<LI>Second item	<LI>Second item
<LI>Third item, etc.	<LI>Third item, etc.
</UL>	</OL>

Variations to first line of list (HTML source):

<UL TYPE=SQUARE>	*square bullets*	<OL TYPE=A>	*capital letters*
<UL TYPE=DISC>	*round bullets*	<OL JYPE=a>	*lower case letters*
<UL TYPE=CIRCLE>	*circle bullets*	<OL TYPE=I>	*Roman capitals*
		<OL TYPE=i>	*Roman numerals*

Task 1: Numbered list

The document used in this task would probably not be posted to an Internet site but would more likely be used in an Intranet situation. An Intranet works like the Internet but restricts access to selected users – for example, within an organisation – and allows organisational documents to be accessible using a browser.

1. Start a new blank Web page and key in the heading as illustrated below. Use *Heading 2* style for the heading and use a horizontal rule to separate the heading from the list.

2. Click on the **Numbering** button in the toolbar and key in the bullet points. Save the document as *Code of Practice.htm*. View using **Web Page Preview**.

3. You may wish to experiment with different types of numbering by reformatting the list using **Format-Bullets and Numbering**.

4. Investigate the underlying source code. Close the document.

Code of Practice

---

1. General
2. Instructions
3. For Sale Boards
4. Published Material
5. Offers
6. Access to Premises
7. Clients' Money
8. Conflict of Interest
9. Financial Services
10. Interpretations and Definitions

Nested lists

Lists can be 'nested', one inside the other, to give several levels of indents (or a multi-level list). When you are nesting lists, you can use bullets for one level and numbers for another. A bulleted outer list and a numbered inner list make an effective combination. Changes in emphasis, using bold, italic and font size, can be used to control the level of prominence of list items. You may create a nested list as follows.

1. Type the entries in your list.

2. Select the list and use **Format-Bullets and Numbering**. It doesn't matter that at this stage all the list items are at the same level.

3. Select the entries you want to nest within the larger list, and then click on the **Increase Indent** button on the toolbar. While these entries are selected you can apply the type of bullet or number you require.

Task 2: A nested list

In this task you will import the text of the document *Code of Practice.doc* into the HTML document created in the last task. There are various lists and multi-level lists in this document.

1. Open both the HTML and Word versions of *Code of Practice*. Using the **Window** menu view the HTML version and add a horizontal rule on a blank line at the end of the numbered list.

2. Switch to the Word document and copy the text and heading of 'General'. Move back to the HTML document and paste. Remove the numbers from the pasted text.

Mark all text and click on the **Numbering** button. Click on each paragraph of text and then in the **Increase Indent** button. Save the HTML document.

3. Expand the *General* section, as illustrated below.

---

1. *General*
   a. This Code applies to estate agency services in the United Kingdom for the selling and buying of residential property.
   b. You must offer equality of professional service to any person, regardless of race, creed, sex or nationality.
   c. You must always act within the law.
   d. You must ensure that you and all members of your staff keep to this Code.

2. *Instructions*
   a. By law you must give your client written confirmation of his instructions to act in the buying or selling of properties on his behalf.

3. *For Sale Boards*
   a. You can only erect a 'For Sale' board with the client's permission. When you put up a 'For Sale' board you must keep to the Town and Country Planning (Control of Advertisements) Regulations 1992 as amended.

4. *Published Material*
   a. You must take all reasonable steps to make sure that all statements, whether oral or written, made about a property are accurate. Whenever possible, the written details of a property must be sent to the Seller for them to confirm that the details are accurate.

---

4. Try changing the numbering style for the first level of numbers to a letter style. When viewed by the browser, you may find that after the second level of bulleting the lettering returns to 'a'. This can be put right directly in the HTML source but after you have done this do not use Word to edit the file. The cure is to remove the *</OL>* tag before the *<UL>* list and the *<OL Type="a">* tag after it. It is better to use multi-level lists that have numbers within bullets unless you wish to edit the source code directly.

5. Bookmark two of the headings and create links to these from the numbered list at the top of the page. Save, preview, test and close the file.

Tables

A table is a compact and readable way of displaying items of information. A table can be used to display text, links, graphics or any other items that can be incorporated into a Web page. Tables can be enhanced with borders, colours and graphics to give more visual impact to the page.

Create a simple table for text as follows:

1. Choose **Table-Insert Table**. This is equivalent to inserting *<TABLE>* and *</TABLE>* tags in your document.

2. Drag across the grid to select the number of rows and columns you need.

3. Type text in the rows and columns of your table. If you want to change the width of your columns, drag column borders with the mouse.

4. Format your table using commands from the **Table-Table Properties** command, which has the following options:

    ❏   Four tabs to determine how other text on the page wraps around your table; the height of rows; the width of columns; and the alignment of cells.

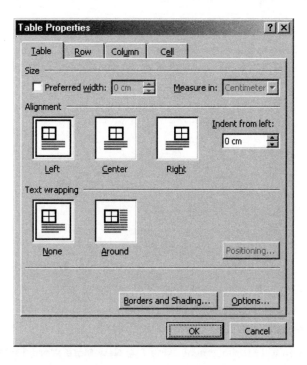

❑ **Borders and Shading** button, to add a border and background shading to the table.

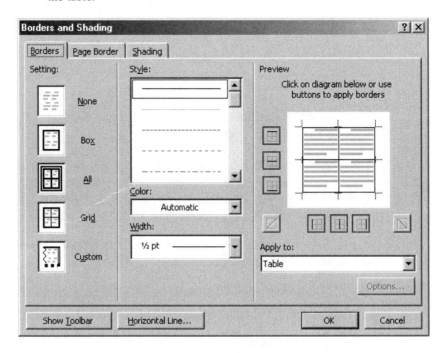

❑ **Options** button, to determine cell margins and spacing.

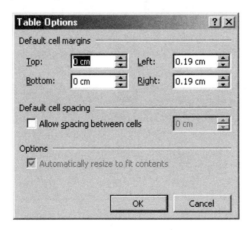

Task 3: Creating a table

1. Open a new HTML document using **File-New-More Word Tables** and choosing *Simple Layout* from the **Web Pages** tab. Delete the sample text.

2. Add the title ***Bishop's Place Development*** using the style *Heading 1*. Save as *Bishop's Place*.

3. Add a table using **Table-Insert-Table** and set this to four columns and five rows. Add the text shown below by copying and pasting from *Price List.doc*.

Bishop's Place Development

Plot No	House Type and Accommodation	Completion Date	Sales Price
3	5 bed detached with double garage	February 2002	£322,500
4	5 bed detached with double garage	February 2002	£327,500
5	5 bed detached with double garage	March 2002	£325,000
6	5 bed detached with triple garage with games room over	March 2002	£355,950

4. Select the first column and centre it, select the last column and right-align it. Mark the whole table and choose **Table-Table properties**, click on the **Cell** tab and choose **Center** for the vertical alignment. Adjust the column widths.

5. Select the top row and using **Format-Borders and Shading** and the **Shading** tab change the background colour of these cells. On the **Borders** tab, increase the width of the borders. Save the changes.

Bishop's Place Development

Plot No	House Type and Accommodation	Completion Date	Sales Price
3	5 bed detached with double garage	February 2002	£322,500
4	5 bed detached with double garage	February 2002	£327,500
5	5 bed detached with double garage	March 2002	£325,000
6	5 bed detached with triple garage with games room over	March 2002	£355,950

6. Experiment with formatting this table in other ways.

    If you save a Word document containing a table as an HTML document, the table will be preserved in the HTML document.

Linking and positioning an image

A graphic that will be displayed in your document when it is loaded into a browser can be added to your HTML document using **Insert-Picture**. This kind of graphic is called an 'in-line graphic', or 'image', and uses the <*IMG*> tag in the source. You should use these types of graphics judiciously, for two reasons:

1. In-line graphics will not automatically be displayed by every browser. Some browsers are unable to display graphics at all, and most browsers allow users to choose not to download graphics in order to increase browsing speed. Therefore, your page should be understandable even if users can't see the graphics. You should always include alternative text (the *ALT* attribute) to display in place of these graphics.

2. The fewer in-line graphics you include, the quicker your file can be downloaded and browsed through. It is good Web publishing practice not to slow down your users with extremely large (or a large number of) in-line graphics. You can speed up your file by reducing the number of colours in your graphics, and also by including *HEIGHT* and *WIDTH* attributes.

In-line graphics are commonly used as decorative elements to make a Web page more attractive, for example to create 'fancy' bullet characters. Another common use is to provide a graphical 'hot spot' that the user clicks in order to activate a hyperlink.

There are two graphics file formats that are used by browsers: GIF files (their extension is *.gif*) and JPG files (their extension is *.jpg*, usually pronounced 'jaypeg'). The GIF file format is typically used for in-line graphics. If you convert an existing Word document that has an in-line graphic in it to HTML form, the graphic will be converted to a GIF file and will be linked to the document automatically. When you use **Insert-Picture** and choose a graphic that is not in this format then it will be converted and the converted graphic file will be stored in the same directory (folder) as the htm file.

You may insert a graphic into your document as follows:

1. Choose **Insert-Picture-From File**. The Insert Picture dialog box appears (as illustrated below).

2. Using the **Look in** box select the directory (folder) in which the graphics file is stored. Select the file from the **Name** box and click on **Insert**. ClipArt can be inserted by choosing **Insert-Picture-Clip Art**.

You may convert an existing document containing an image to HTML format as follows:

1. Create the document you wish to convert using the Normal template. Add graphics or create your own using **Insert-Object-Microsoft Word picture**. If

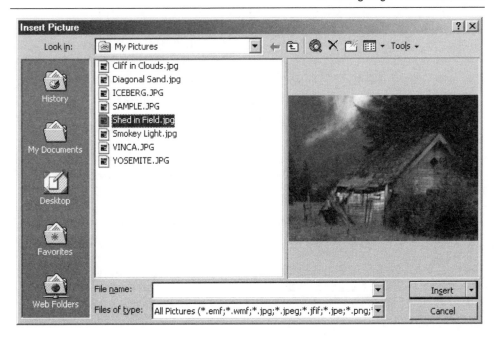

you want to add WordArt then use **Insert-Object-Microsoft Word picture** and then **Insert-Picture-WordArt** to create the WordArt in the picture workspace.

2. Choose **File-Save As HTML**.

Aligning and sizing an image

An image on its own on a line may be centred or left-aligned, as for text. If the image and text are used on the same line then, by default, text is aligned with the bottom of the image.

If text wrapping is required then select the image and use **Format-Picture**. Under the **Layout** tab (see below) the style of text wrapping can be selected.

Usually, graphics are displayed at their natural size, but you can alter the size of a graphic by dragging the sizing handles. This will define, in pixels, the *HEIGHT* and *WIDTH* attributes in the source code *<IMG>* tag. These attributes are included in the *<IMG>* tag, as shown in the following example:

    <IMG SRC="IMAGE1 GIF" HEIGHT=90 WIDTH=90>

If the viewer of your page has a browser that cannot display your picture then an alternative text caption can be provided using the Format Picture dialog box. Click on the **Web** tab and type your caption into the **Alternative Text** box.

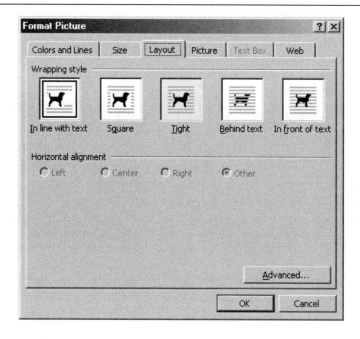

Task 4: Adding an image

1. Open the HTML document *Bishop's Place* and add some WordArt as follows.

2. Choose **Insert-Object-Microsoft Word picture**. Use **Insert-Picture-WordArt** to create some WordArt with formatting of your choice for the text 'Bishop's Place' in the picture workspace.

3. Reset the boundary of the picture workspace and click on **Close Picture**. Adjust the size of the WordArt to fit across the top of the page and save. This will convert the image into a graphics file that can be viewed by a browser.

    The HTML page with the added image is shown below.

Bishop's Place

Bishop's Place Development

Plot No	House Type and Accommodation	Completion Date	Sales Price
3	5 bed detached with double garage	February 2002	£322,500
4	5 bed detached with double garage	February 2002	£327,500
5	5 bed detached with double garage	March 2002	£325,000
6	5 bed detached with triple garage with games room over	March 2002	£355,950

Background images

A background to your Web page can be produced from a graphic that is repeated on the screen in a wallpapered or tiled effect. It may be a company logo and is usually created in faint pastel colours so that foreground text and graphics are not masked by it. Word offers a number of different textured backgrounds, which can be added using the Fill Effects dialog box as follows:

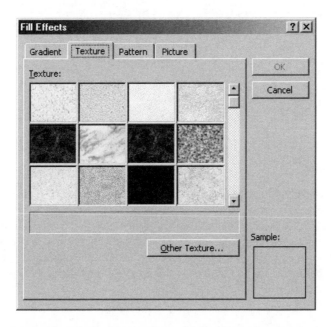

1. Choose **Format-Background-Fill Effects** to open the Fill Effects dialog box. Click on the **Texture** tab, from which a textured background can be chosen. If you just want a plain colour, select from the background palette after selecting **Format-Background**.

2. If you want to use your own graphic as textured wallpaper then click on the **Other Texture** button and select the file you require.

Text and link colours

You can specify the colour in which text will be displayed, as well as the colour of visited (followed) and unvisited hyperlinks (*TEXT*, *VLINK* and *LINK* attributes, respectively). To change the hyperlink colours use **Format-Style**, click on **Hyperlink** or **FollowedHyperlink** and then on **Modify**. Change the format as you would for any other style.

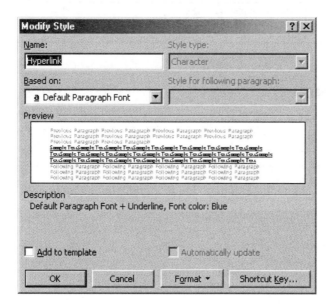

Images for bullets

As you probably noticed when the bulleted list was considered earlier in this unit, Word offers a choice of small graphics for bullets. If one of these is chosen, an image tag *<IMG>* is added before the text of the point, and the list tags as described earlier are not used. If you have created your own images that you wish to use as bullet points then click on the **Picture** button under the **Bulleted** tab of the Bullets and Numbering dialog box to display the Picture Bullet dialog box (see below).

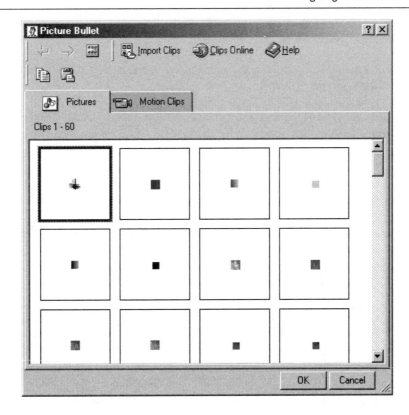

Images and links

You can also include graphics in your HTML documents using hyperlinks. Hyperlinked graphics don't show up when your document is downloaded; the user accesses them by activating a hyperlink. This is the preferred method for linking to graphics that are very large or important.

Images themselves can be used to invoke links in the same way as for the usual text links. Using this technique your page could contain a menu of fancy buttons, which you could create using WordArt; when clicked, these would invoke a link to another page.

Task 5: Links to images

In the Estate Agency application you could make pictures of properties available on the Web pages. By using links to these pictures, viewers can elect whether or not to look at the picture, if the property interests them, and do not have to wait for pictures to download which they do not want to see. You can investigate this effect by using an impression of a house to be built on Plot 5 at Bishop's Place. Using Microsoft Paint or another drawing or painting program, create a simple image , saving it in GIF format as *House.gif*.

1. Move the file *House.gif* to the same directory as that in which you have the document *Bishop's Place*.

2. Open the HTML document *Bishop's Place* and select the text **5 bed detached with double garage** in the first row in the table.

3. Choose **Insert-Hyperlink** and click on the **File** button. In the **Files of type** box select **Internet files** and select the directory in which *House.gif* is stored. Highlight this file, click on **OK** and click on **OK** again.

Bishop's Place Development

Plot No	House Type and Accommodation	Completion Date	Sales Price
3	5 bed detached with double garage	February 2002	£322,500
4	5 bed detached with double garage	February 2002	£327,500
5	5 bed detached with double garage	March 2002	£325,000
6	5 bed detached with triple garage with games room over	March 2002	£355,950

4. Test out this link. When clicked it will display the image on its own and the viewer can use the browser's **Back** button to return to the price list page.

Task 6: Images as links

In visiting Web sites, you will probably have noticed that pages often contain images that you can click on to link to another page. In this task we will create some WordArt saying 'Home page' that will be used as a link to the home page.

1. Open the HTML document *Bishop's Place* and move to the end of the document.

2. Choose **Insert-Object-Microsoft Word Picture**. Select **Insert-Picture-WordArt** and choose a style for your WordArt.

3. Type in the text **Home Page** and choose a font and size for your WordArt. Choose a size of around 14 points as you don't want the link to be too big.

4. Set the picture boundary and close the picture. Save the document in order to save the WordArt as an image.

5. Select the picture and choose **Insert-Hyperlink**, browse for the file *homepage.htm* (created in Unit 18) and select it as the link. Save and test out the link.

Plot No	House Type and Accommodation	Completion Date	Sales Price
3	5 bed detached with double garage	February 2002	£322,500
4	5 bed detached with double garage	February 2002	£327,500
5	5 bed detached with double garage	March 2002	£325,000
6	5 bed detached with triple garage with games room over	March 2002	£355,950

Sound and video

Sound

You can have a background sound play automatically when someone opens your Web page.

1. Display the **Web Tools** toolbar and click on the **Sound** button.

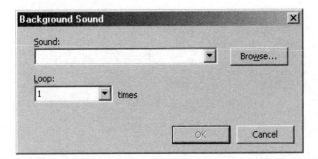

2. In the **Background Sound** box, enter the address or URL of the sound file you want or click on **Browse** to locate the file.

3. In the **Loop** box, click the number of times you want the sound to repeat. If you want it to loop continually while the Web page is open, click **Infinite**.

To turn the sound on or off while you are creating the Web page, click on the **Design Mode** button.

Remember that visitors to your Web site will only be able to hear background sounds if they have a sound system installed and their Web browser supports the sound format of the file you inserted. Common sound file formats are WAV MID, AU, AIF, RMI, SND and MP2 (MPEG audio).

As the background sound plays automatically every time your page is opened or returned to, your visitors could find it annoying. For the same reason you should exercise caution when selecting **Infinite** for a sound-looping option. You might be better adding the background sound to one of your pages that is visited less often. As with large graphics, you could insert a hyperlink so that the user can click on a link to download a sound file.

Video

You can add an in-line video to your Web page, which means the video will be downloaded when the user opens the page. You can determine whether the video will play when the page is opened or when the user points to the video with the mouse. Because not all Web browsers support in-line video you may want to provide alternative text and images or avoid presenting essential information in videos.

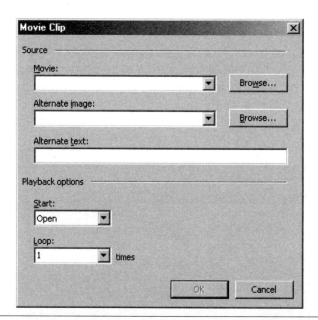

1. Display the **Web Tools** toolbar and click on the **Movie** button.

2. In the **Movie** box under **Source**, type the address or URL of the video file you want or click on the **Browse** button to search for the file.

3. In the **Alternate image** box, type the address or URL of the graphics file that you want to designate as a substitute when the viewer's browser doesn't support videos or when the viewer turns off the display of videos.

4. In the **Alternate text** box, type the text that you want to appear in place of the video.

5. In the **Start** list, click an option to specify how the video will play on a Web page. **Open** causes the video to play when the user downloads the Web page; **Mouse-over** causes the video to play when the pointer moves over the video; **Both** causes the video to play in both scenarios.

6. In the **Loop** box, enter the number of times you want the video to repeat. If you want to display video controls such as 'Start' and 'Stop' while you're authoring Web pages, tick the **Display video controls** check box.

Note that the video will play after you insert it. If you've selected the **Mouse-over** option for video playback, the video will also play in your Web page document when your mouse moves over it.

Video files can be very large and take a long time to download. Therefore, it is advisable to insert a hyperlink to a video, so that the viewer can click the hyperlink to download the video and play it.

Forms and Feedback in HTML Documents

What you will learn in this unit

A form incorporated into an HTML document provides a means for viewers to interact with you through your pages. An HTML form is created in much the same way as an on-line form, incorporating GUI features such as check boxes, radio (option) buttons and drop-down lists that are familiar features of dialog boxes.

Unlike other aspects of HTML, forms involve two-way communication and will only function if your service provider runs software to pick up the responses. You will need to sort out how and where your responses will be stored so that you can retrieve them for analysis.

A form can be created in a separate document or it can be included as part of a larger page. All formatting that can be used in an HTML document can be used in a form, and the tags that collect data and send the form provide the interactivity.

A form is enclosed by the *<FORM>* and *</FORM>* tags. Within the form, data is collected by text boxes, tick boxes, option groups and drop-down lists, all of which are implemented by *<INPUT...>* tags.

At the end of this unit you will be able to:

❑ Create forms in an HTML document.

❑ Add controls to HTML forms.

What you need

To complete this unit you will need:

❑ The document template *Customer details form* created in Unit 14

The Web Tools

The Web Tools toolbar allows you to add controls to the form in a similar way to that for on-line forms. The buttons allow you to create a form field and define options for it. There are also additional buttons for the extra features in HTML forms. Some of these are introduced in the tasks in this unit.

To add controls to a form you need to be in Form Design mode. The document will switch into design mode as you add controls from the the toolbox to it, but you can switch between Form Design Mode and the normal editing mode by clicking on the **Design Mode** button.

Sending the form

You can add a button to the form so that your viewers can click on it to send their responses. Clicking on the **Submit** button in the Control Toolbox will create a button which, when clicked by the viewer, will send the form's contents back to you.

Submission information

You may need to specify the properties of the **Submit** button and these are briefly summarised below:

Action   Specifies the URL of the script on your server to which you want to submit the contents of the form. If you do not specify an Action, the default is the current document.

Encoding   This attribute specifies the format of the form's data. The default value of Encoding is *application/x-www-form-urlencoded*.

Method   The Method property specifies the way data is submitted. The default Method is *Get*.

You should contact your system administrator or service provider for specific information relating to forms.

Reset

To clear a form, a reset button that clears the form's contents can be provided so that if the viewer wants to start again they can clear all inputs. Clicking on the **Reset** button of the Web Tools will add a button to the form to clear all fields.

Task 1: Creating a simple feedback form

This task creates a simple form requesting a viewer's name, e-mail address and phone number. The form as seen in Form Design Mode is illustrated below.

Top of Form

Feedback Form

We would like to follow up your enquiry, please send us your details.

Name:

E-mail address:

Telephone No.

Submit   Reset

Bottom of Form

1. Start a new document, adding a heading (using style *Heading 2*) entitled **Feedback Form**. Add a horizontal rule and save the document as *Feedback.htm*. Choose **File-Properties** to give the form the title **Simple Form**.

2. Add the text **We would like to follow up your enquiry, please send us your details**.

3. Turn on the display of the Web Tools tolbar and switch to Design Mode. Type in **Name:** and click on the **Textbox** button. A text box field will be added to the form. Click on the **Properties** button and set **HTMLName** as *Lastname*. (Note you do not have to set this property but it may make it easier to identify the feedback data.) If you wish to alter the size of the text box controls, return to Form Design Mode, drag its sizing handles to make it the size you require.

197

4. On a new line, key in the text **E-mail address:** and click on the **Textbox** button. Display the properties and key in **Email** as the **HTMLName** of the field.

5. Make the next line one for the viewer to key in their telephone number. Give the **HTMLName Phone** to the text box field and use the default settings.

6. Next add the **Submit** and **Reset** buttons simply by clicking on the **Submit** and **Reset** buttons in the Web Tools toolbar. Add appropriate properties for the **Submit** button.

7. Save the form. It is now ready for use. Exit Design Mode to test the form.

When a viewer completes the form and clicks on the **Submit** button, the data they have entered will be passed to you by your Internet service provider. The data that you receive may be of the form:

Lastname=Other&Email=a.n.other@univ.ac.uk&Phone=01234567890

Alternatively, it may be processed so that you receive it in a form suitable for importing into a database or spreadsheet. Check with your system administrator or service provider to identify the format.

Adding controls

As well as text boxes, you can add check boxes, radio buttons, text areas and drop-down lists to your forms.

Check boxes and radio (option group) buttons

Some responses may be of a simple yes/no nature: for example, 'Do you require a brochure?' A check box is a useful way of providing yes/no alternatives. You may also wish to specify an option group where several choices are offered but you only want to allow the viewer to choose one: these are known as radio buttons. A check box is square and a radio button is round.

A check box is added by clicking on the **Check box** button in the Web Tools. If the viewer selects the check box, the data that is returned is set to 'on' (true) as opposed to 'off' (false) for not checked. If no default value for the check box is specified then the check box is initially assigned the value of *off* (not checked).

With radio buttons, the same name should be used for all the radios in the set, as you only want to allow one of the alternatives to be chosen. (If you only want to use one set you could leave the name blank but it is likely to be useful to label the returned answers.)

You should also set a different **Value** property for each radio button. It is usual to number them but other 'values' may be chosen. If the *Checked* property for each radio button is left as *False*, then all the buttons will be empty when the form is

first opened. If you want to provide a default choice then set the *Checked* property to *True* for the option you wish to be checked by default.

Task 2: Check boxes and option groups

In this task you will create a section of the on-line form from Unit 14. Later you will add to this form to create a complete HTML version.

1. Start a new document, add a heading (use style *Heading 3*) entitled **Type of property you are interested in** and add a horizontal rule. Save the document as *Property enquiry.htm*. Display the Web Tools toolbar and turn on Design Mode.

2. Add a table three columns by two rows and complete it as illustrated below, inserting the check boxes using the **Check box** button in the Web Tools. You may add HTML names, using the same names as the label. If you wish, you may border the table.

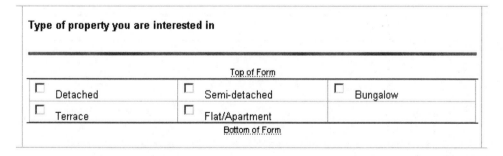

3. Under this an option group can be added to allow the user to select from the options Leasehold/Freehold/either. Add another row to the table (you may differentiate this by suitable use of bordering) and add the text and option buttons as illustrated below. Set the **HTMLName** for each button and set the **Value** to *1*, *2* and *3* for each button respectively. Save the form.

Type of property you are interested in

Top of Form

☐ Detached	☐ Semi-detached	☐ Bungalow
☐ Terrace	☐ Flat/Apartment	
○ Leasehold	○ Freehold	○ Leasehold or Freehold

Bottom of Form

Text area controls

The text box control only accepts one line of text and is defined by the HTML source *<INPUT...>* tag. If you want to allow your viewer to enter several lines, for example to provide you with their comments, use the **Textarea** control in the Web Tools (implemented in HTML source by *<TEXTAREA...>* and </TEXTAREA> tags). The text area can be sized using its sizing handles.

Drop-down lists

A drop-down list is a neat way of offering a set of alternatives as we have seen for an on-line form. They are added by clicking on the **Dropdown Box** control in the Web Tools (implemented in HTML source using *<SELECT...>* and *<OPTION...>*).

Task 3: Adding a text area and drop-down list to the form

Type of property you are interested in

Top of Form

☐ Detached	☐ Semi-detached	☐ Bungalow
☐ Terrace	☐ Flat/Apartment	
○ Leasehold	○ Freehold	○ Leasehold or Freehold

If there are any further details you would like to give us to aid our search for suitable properties please use the space below:

Bottom of Form

1. Continuing with the *Property enquiry* form, add a text area to the bottom of the form as illustrated above. Drag the text area box to the size that you require. You could add an extra row to the table and merge the cells to give room for the text area. Use an **HTMLname**: for example, ***addinfo***. Save the form.

2. A drop-down list is used to select the person's title, i.e. Mr, Mrs etc. At the top of the form, insert another 3-column table. Type ***Title:*** and click on the **Dropdown Box** button. Click on the **Properties** button and in the **DisplayValues** property type the list of values you want, separating each with a semi-colon: e.g. *Mr;Mrs;Miss;Ms;Mr &Mrs;Dr*. Set the **HTMLName** to *Title*.

An example of how this might look is shown below. Save the form.

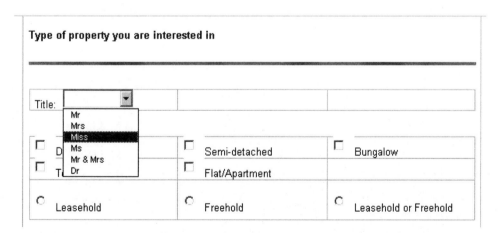

3. Add text boxes for the address and check boxes for the price ranges. Why is it better to use check boxes for these than option buttons? Copy the logo from the *Customer details form* template. Finish the form, as shown below.

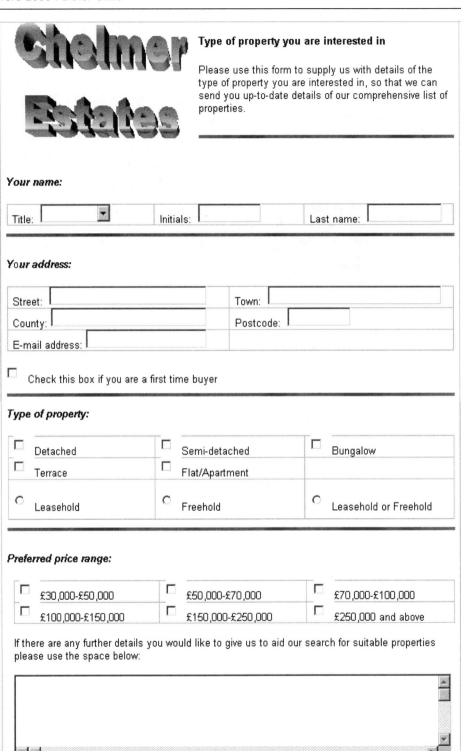

Type of property you are interested in

Please use this form to supply us with details of the type of property you are interested in, so that we can send you up-to-date details of our comprehensive list of properties.

Your name:

Title:	Initials:	Last name:

Your address:

Street:	Town:
County:	Postcode:
E-mail address:	

☐ Check this box if you are a first time buyer

Type of property:

☐ Detached	☐ Semi-detached	☐ Bungalow
☐ Terrace	☐ Flat/Apartment	
○ Leasehold	○ Freehold	○ Leasehold or Freehold

Preferred price range:

☐ £30,000-£50,000	☐ £50,000-£70,000	☐ £70,000-£100,000
☐ £100,000-£150,000	☐ £150,000-£250,000	☐ £250,000 and above

If there are any further details you would like to give us to aid our search for suitable properties please use the space below:

4. Add **Submit** and **Reset** buttons and save the form. Exit Design Mode to test the form.

Thank you for your co-operation. Please send us your details by clicking on this button [Submit]

To clear all entries in the form click on this button [Reset]

Analysing feedback

Data may be returned to you in a variety of ways depending on your Internet service provider. The data may be simple text strings or in a form that can be imported into a database. Once data has been imported into a database, it can be queried, counted, sorted and grouped in answer to the questions posed in the form. You will find using the **HTMLName** property useful as these names correspond to field names in your database of answers.

By combining the information given in previous units, you can create sophisticated Web pages for a variety of uses.

Customising Word

Tools-Options

Word can be customised to suit a particular user or the circumstances in which it is being used. This appendix investigates the options available from the **Tools-Options** command. These options are grouped into the following categories:

View	**General**
Edit	**Print**
Save	**Spelling and grammar**
Track changes	**User information**
Compatibility	**File locations**

Not all of these will be discussed: only those options which it is considered the reader may wish to change. To use any of the other options consult the help information to be sure that you know the effect of any change you make.

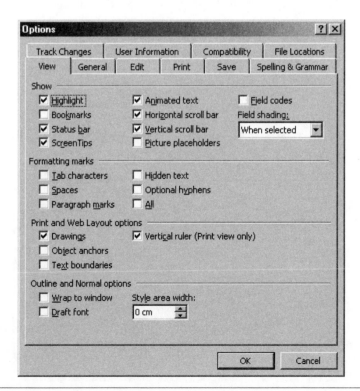

View

In this category the options available affect the window display, text and non-printing characters.

By clicking in the appropriate check boxes, you can choose whether or not to display the scrollbars and the status bar.

If, in Normal view, the **Style area width** is increased from its default value of zero, the document is displayed with a left margin showing the style name applied to the corresponding text.

It is best to leave the **Formatting marks** options as their default values. There may be occasions when hidden characters such as paragraph marks are required to be seen. However, you will usually switch these on or off with the ¶ button.

General

Here you can alter the measurement units that Word uses. You may choose between centimetres, millimetres, inches, points and picas. You can also specify the number of recently opened files that will be displayed on the **File** menu.

Edit

The one setting you may wish to alter is that of **Typing replaces selection**, particularly if you are new to Word. New users of Word can make selections by

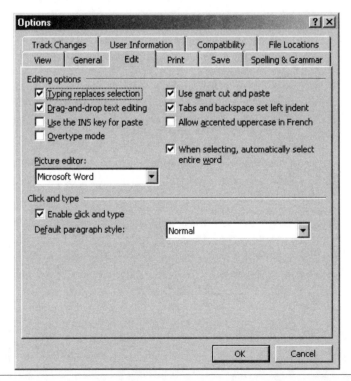

mistake and if this is followed by, say, pressing *Enter* then the selection disappears. (It has been replaced by a paragraph mark.) **Edit-Undo** will remedy this but a new user might not recognise what has happened soon enough. If this option is switched off, by clicking in the check box to remove the tick, then this problem is avoided.

Other settings in this category which you may wish to alter are the operation of the drag and drop feature or the selection of text in units of whole words.

Print

The option in this section you may wish to use is **Reverse print order**. This will cause a document to be printed from the last page to the first, which is useful if your printer places each sheet face up, so that they end up back to front.

Save

Here it is possible to choose fast saving and creating an automatic backup of your document. If you choose to create a backup copy, you will get a *.bak* version of your document each time you save (the previous backup is overwritten each time). However, it is better simply to get into the habit of saving your work every few minutes.

Word also provides an AutoRecovery feature that will regularly save the document. The AutoRecovery version of the file is loaded when you start Word follow a crash of the system. You can adjust the time interval between saves.

Sensitive documents may be password-protected but be cautious using this.

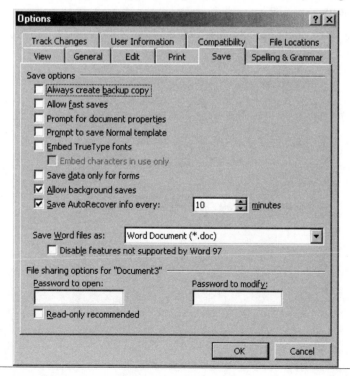

Spelling and Grammar

Word can be customised so that it checks spelling and grammar as you type, depending on these options. Options may be set to allow the spell checker to ignore words that are in upper case, words that contain numbers, etc.

Clicking on the **Dictionaries** button allows you to set up your own dictionary. The **Always suggest corrections** box may be used to speed up checking (checking is quicker if this is switched off). Also, you may choose to check spelling from the main dictionary only.

Track Changes

These options determine the appearance of changes when the tracking feature is turned on (**Tools-Track Changes**).

User Information

Enter your name, initials and address here. Your name is stored with the document each time it is saved.

Compatibility

These options are used if you want to make Word behave like some other word processor (not recommended).

File Locations

The **File Locations** tab allows you to specify the location of specific groups of files.

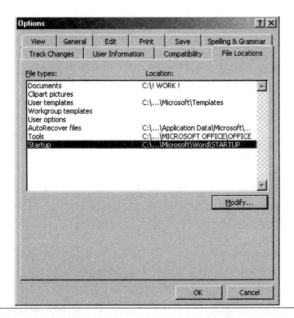

In particular, it is worth setting the **Start** directory to be the folder where you usually store you Word documents. This folder will then be suggested as the default the first time you open or save a document in each Word session.

Customising toolbars

If you find you use a command often, you might want to set up the toolbars so they have precisely the buttons you want to use: for example, adding a button to the Standard toolbar.

To add a button to a toolbar:

1. Choose **View-Toolbars-Customize**.

2. Click on the **Commands** tab, and select a category that includes the button you want to add. The buttons, with their descriptions, appear on the right in a scrollable list box.

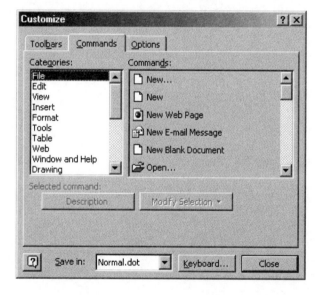

3. When you find the button you want to add, drag it and drop it on the toolbar where you want it (at the top of the Word window).

4. Click on Close when you have finished making changes.

You can create your own toolbar by clicking on **New** on the **Toolbars** tab.

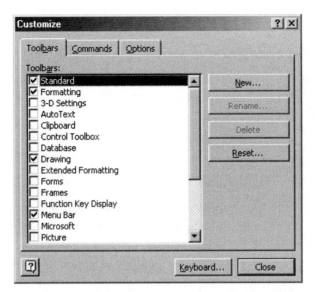

Index